Campaign

# The Yom Kippur War 1973 (1)

## The Golan Heights

Campaign • 118

OSPREY
PUBLISHING

# The Yom Kippur War 1973 (1)

## The Golan Heights

Simon Dunstan • Illustrated by Howard Gerrard

Series editor Lee Johnson • Consultant editor David G Chandler

First published in Great Britain in 2003 by Osprey Publishing, Elms Court,
Chapel Way, Botley, Oxford OX2 9LP, United Kingdom.
Email: info@ospreypublishing.com

A CIP catalogue record for this book is available from the British Library

ISBN 1 84176 220 2

Editor: Lee Johnson
Design: The Black Spot
Index by Alison Worthington
Maps by The Map Studio
3D bird's-eye views by The Black Spot
Battlescene artwork by Howard Gerrard
'The Battlefield Today' by Marsh Gelbart
Originated by Grasmere Digital Imaging, Leeds, UK
Printed in China through World Print Ltd.

04 05 06 07   10 9 8 7 6 5 4 3 2

For a catalogue of all books published by Osprey Military
and Aviation please contact:

Osprey Direct UK, P.O. Box 140, Wellingborough,
Northants, NN8 2FA, UK
E-mail: info@ospreydirect.co.uk

Osprey Direct USA, c/o MBI Publishing, P.O. Box 1,
729 Prospect Ave, Osceola, WI 54020, USA
E-mail: info@ospreydirectusa.com

www.ospreypublishing.com

# Dedication

Dr. Randalf G.S. Cooper

# Acknowledgements

Mahmoud Bahri, US Department of Defense, Sgalit
Har-Arie, LtCol David Eshel, Marsh Gelbart, Office of the
IDF Spokesperson, Jerusalem Post, Samuel M. Katz,
Tamzin LeBlanc, Abraham Rabinovitch, Col Yizhar Sahar,
MajGen Heikki Tilander, United Nations, Steven J. Zaloga.

# Artist's note

Readers may care to note that the original paintings from
which the colour plates in this book were prepared are
available for private sale. All reproduction copyright
whatsoever is retained by the Publishers. All enquiries
should be addressed to:

Howard Gerrard
11 Oaks Road
Tenterden
Kent
TN30 6RD
UK

The Publishers regret that they can enter into no
correspondence upon this matter.

# Editor's note

This is a the first of two volumes examining the events of
the Yom Kippur War of October 1973. The twin volume
detailing the fighting in the Sinai is Campaign 126 *The Yom
Kippur War 1973 (2) The Sinai*.

## KEY TO MILITARY SYMBOLS

# CONTENTS

A classic image of armoured warfare illustrates the principle of employing tanks en masse as a formation of *Sho't* Upgraded Centurions advances on Syrian positions. It also shows the normal posture of Israeli tank commanders in battle and how exposed they were to enemy fire, be it exploding artillery shells or Syrian snipers who were deployed on the battlefield with their Dragunov rifles with the specific task of killing Israeli tank commanders.

# BACKGROUND TO WAR

President Hafaz al Assad of Syria. Born in 1924 of the Alawite clan, Assad joined the ruling Ba'ath Party in 1958 and rose to become the commander of the Syrian Air Force. He was subsequently the Minister of Defence during the Six Day War. He seized supreme power in October 1970 and began to rebuild the Syrian Armed Forces for the coming battle with Israel that erupted in October 1973.

On the afternoon of 10 June 1967, a ceasefire imposed by the United Nations brought an end to the Arab-Israeli Six Day War. The ceasefire found the Israel Defense Forces (IDF) triumphant on the Suez Canal, on the Jordan River, and on the Golan Heights, some 26km (16 miles) east of the old frontier with Syria. The entire Sinai, the Gaza Strip, the West Bank including East Jerusalem, and the troublesome Golan Heights were now in Israeli hands. In less than a week the IDF conquered an area three and a half times that of Israel itself, as well as over 1,000,000 Palestinians living in the West Bank and Gaza Strip. In six days the geopolitical balance in the Middle East was radically altered. Three sovereign Arab states, Egypt, Jordan and Syria, were utterly humiliated. Early in August 1967, Arab leaders met in Khartoum where they rejected any form of negotiation with Israel and resolved to reclaim the lost lands through force of arms. (See Campaign 126 *The Yom Kippur War 1973 (2) The Sinai* for the political background to the conflict.)

With the death of Gamal Abdel Nasser in September 1970, his successor, President Anwar Sadat, carefully reconstructed the Egyptian armed forces over the following years. At the same time he persuaded President Hafaz al Assad of Syria to adopt his strategy of a military campaign with achievable aims. The aim would be to win a substantial lodgement across the Suez Canal in the Sinai Desert and the recapture of the Golan Heights prior to a United Nations ceasefire that would break the diplomatic logjam and focus the world's attention on the Middle East once more. Both countries conducted a brilliant deception plan, codenamed Operation Spark, to lull the Israelis into a false sense of security prior to their joint offensive on two fronts.

# OPPOSING PLANS

errain is significant in any military operation but on the Golan it was fundamental both to the attackers and defenders and to a large extent determined the dispositions and plans of both sides. Rising above the Jordan Valley from the Sea of Galilee is an escarpment some 1,000m high known as the Golan Heights. Covering an area of about 900 square kilometres, it rises steadily from south to north; its peaks looking down on the Upper Jordan Valley to the west and the Yarmouk Valley to the south. The latter forms the boundary with Jordan, which to the east gives way to extensive lava fields. In the distant past, this rugged terrain was shaped by volcanic activity. Lava, belching from craters, covered the high plateau with a coating of basalt. The largest volcanic cones such as Tel Faris, rise to over 1,000m above sea level. Dominating the northern end of the Golan is the peak of Mount Hermon, called Jebel Sheikh by the Arabs. This strategic high ground with its vital observation post was known as 'The Eyes of Israel' as it dominated the surrounding terrain with excellent views of much of the northern Golan and deep into Syria.

In contrast to the Sinai in the south, the Golan is not good tank country. The going is better in the southern grasslands than in the north where large areas are rendered impassable to vehicles by basalt boulders and rock outcrops, while the Golan's many defiles represent perfect ambush country. The volcanic cones scattered across the heights also provide excellent observation posts and fields of fire. Many of them were

A solitary Centurion *Sho't* takes up position behind a wall of basalt rocks. Tank crews use any fold in the ground to minimise exposure to enemy observation or fire. This was particularly significant in the southern area of the Golan Heights with its open rolling terrain. At the outset of the battle, this was defended by just 33 *Sho't* tanks of the 53rd Mechanised Infantry Battalion commanded by Lieutenant Colonel Oded Erez against a force of some 900 Syrian tanks. This unit's ordeal in the October War is one of the most harrowing and courageous in the annals of modern warfare.

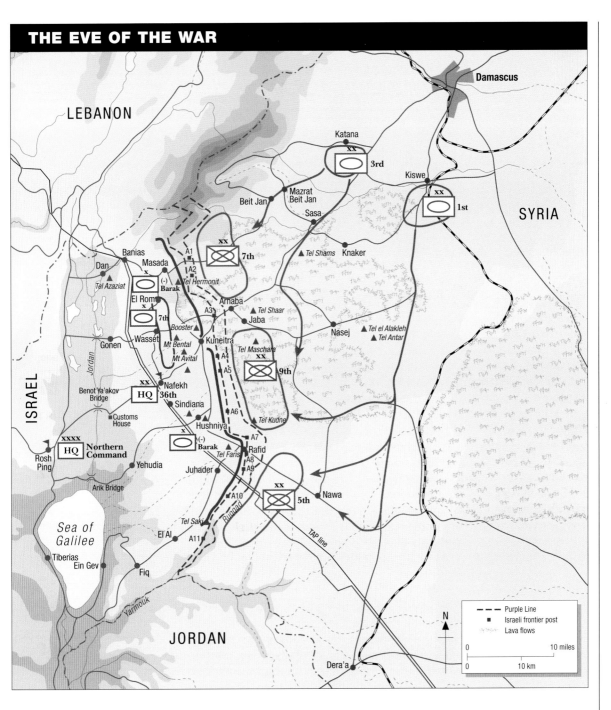

integrated into the Israeli defence system on the Golan as natural firing ramps. Two of the dominant volcanic cones in particular, the 1,200m Mount Hermonit north of Kuneitra and the 1,250m Tel Faris near the Rafid junction, were to play key roles in the October War.

The eastern boundary of the Golan, facing the Damascus Plain, ran in an irregular line along the edge of the United Nations' 'Purple Line' – a demilitarised zone established after the Six Day War and so called because of its colouring on the maps of the UN observers stationed there. Along the ceasefire line there was a narrow strip of neutral territory, less

An M50 155mm SP howitzer fires in support of an Israeli attack on the Golan. One of the major lessons of the October War to all armies was the prodigious scale of ammunition expenditure during the heavy fighting. Artillery and mortars were quickly integrated into the fire plans of Israeli offensive operations to counter the menace of RPG and Sagger anti-tank teams who found plenty of cover among the rocks of the Golan Heights to ambush Israeli tanks.

than 500m wide, patrolled by personnel from the 16 UN observer posts built within the zone.

A number of roads crossed the plateau and there was a network of tracks made by the IDF to aid the movement of military vehicles. There were two north–south roads. The first, set back from the Purple Line, ran for some 75km from Rafid in the south to Masada in the north. The second north–south road ran parallel to the 2,500km underground Trans-Arabian Pipeline (TAP), which carried oil from Saudi Arabia through Jordan across the Golan and into Lebanon where it terminated at the Mediterranean port of Sidon. The maintenance road, the TAP line road to the east of the pipeline, ran inside a chain-link fence. Running from west to east across the Golan were five roads that followed the easiest paths through the broken terrain from bridges over the River Jordan. The capture of these bridges was the principal objective for the Syrian Army in the October War.

After the Six Day War, the Israelis built a system of obstacles and fortifications along the eastern edge of the Golan plateau. To the west of the Purple Line was an anti-tank ditch, approximately six metres wide and four metres deep. On the western side, the spoil from the ditch was piled up to create an embankment shielding a network of concrete observation posts and strongpoints – 'Mutzavim' – built on volcanic hills or high ground, which afforded commanding views over the eastern approaches. There were a total of 17 of these fortified positions, strung out at four-kilometre intervals, each garrisoned by 10–30 troops, as well as intelligence and artillery personnel. Most of the positions were supported by a platoon of three tanks.

The number of infantry stationed on the Golan was commonly two battalions with one to the north of Kuneitra and the other to the south. Positioned about 2,000m to the rear were tanks and behind them four batteries of self-propelled artillery guns – a total of just 44 155mm howitzers. Their main role was to block roads and tracks and to bring down fire on the killing grounds into which Syrian armour and infantry were to be channelled by the minefields and terrain. In a measure much favoured by the IDF, special ramps specifically designed for the Centurion's ten-degree gun depression had been built on higher ground to enable the defending tanks to engage Syrian attackers from long range.

Behind the infantry defences along the Purple Line was the regular garrison brigade for the Golan, the 188th Barak [Lightning] Armoured Brigade with two tank and one mechanised infantry battalions. The brigade was commanded by Colonel Yitzhak Ben Shoham with its head-quarters at Camp *Sa'ar* [Storm] near Nafekh. The two tank battalions of the Barak Brigade possessed some 72 Upgraded Centurions, known within the Israeli Armoured Corps as the *Sho't* [Whip]. These were deployed in support of the forward strongpoints along the Purple Line and, in times of tension, on the firing ramps to the rear.

Israel's overall strategy was simple – survival. It became an article of faith that military intelligence would give sufficient warning for the citizen army of Israel to be mobilised before war erupted. Thereafter, the aim was to mount a counter-offensive within 48 hours and take the battle to the enemy's territory in order to inflict heavy human and material losses to deter further attacks and preserve the integrity of the territories already occupied by Israel. In an area of approximately 48 x 24 km (30 x 15 miles) there was little margin for error. It was a fine judgement as to how many troops and tanks should be stationed on the Golan to stem a Syrian invasion before the reserves could be mobilised, which would take approximately 72 hours. Too many was a waste of resources and a drain on the over-stretched economy and too few a recipe for disaster.

The plan of attack devised by the Syrians was heavily influenced by Soviet military doctrine – the accumulated result of 15 years of Soviet logistical and technical support and the schooling of Syrian officers at Soviet military academies. The aim was to capture the entire Golan Heights and reach the River Jordan within 36 hours. This was to be achieved by the

**Centurions take up hulldown positions among the basalt rocks of the Golan. Experience had shown that the torsion bar suspension systems of the M-48 and M-60 tanks of US origin were less capable than the Centurion or *Sho't* over the rocky terrain of the Golan Heights. Accordingly, only Centurions and Shermans were deployed on the Golan Heights with the M-48 and M-60 *Magach* employed on the Southern Front although a few special-purpose variants, such as the M-48 AVLB Bridgelayer, were used on the Northern Front.**

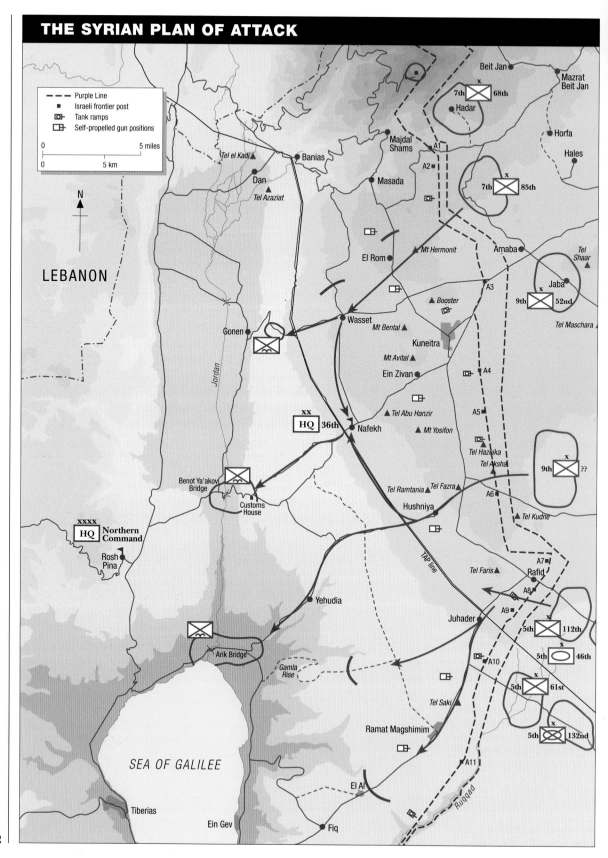

Purple Line
Israeli frontier post
Tank ramps
Self-propelled gun positions

0        5 miles
0        5 km

N

LEBANON

Beit Jan

Mazrat
Beit Jan

7th ☒ 68th
Hadar

Horfa

Hales

Majdal
Shams        A1

A2

7th ☒ 85th

Tel el Kadi ▲    Banias

Dan

Tel Azaziat

Masada

Arnaba                Tel
                       Shaar

Mt Hermonit            A3

El Rom                           Jaba
                            9th ☒ 52nd

Booster                      Tel Maschara

Wasset
Gonen        Mt Bental ▲

            Kuneitra

Jordan      Mt Avital ▲

            Ein Zivan        A4

                             A5

xx
HQ  36th        Tel Abu Hanzir
            Nafekh    ▲ Mt Yosifon

                        Tel Hazeika    9th ☒ ??
                        Tel Aksha

Benot Ya'akov
Bridge

Customs     Tel Ramtania ▲  ▲ Tel Fazra    A6
House

xxxx                 Hushniya              Tel Kudne
HQ  Northern
    Command

Rosh
Pina                                       A7
                                    Tel Faris ▲   Rafid
                            TAP line              A8

                                                  A9
Yehudia

                        Juhader
                                         A10
                                                  5th ☒ 112th

Arik Bridge                                       5th ◯ 46th

        Gamla
        Rise                                      5th ☒ 61st

                        Tel Saki ▲

                    Ramat Magshimim              5th ☒ 132nd

SEA OF GALILEE                          A11

                        El Al

Tiberias

Ein Gev                 Fiq                Ruqqad

onslaught of three infantry and two armoured divisions, although the infantry divisions were heavily reinforced by an independent armoured brigade each as well as a significant mechanised infantry component.

The attack on the Golan was to be preceded by a short but intense bombardment delivered by all the available combat aircraft, artillery, tanks and heavy mortars. Moving forward on a broad front, to make their numerical superiority tell, the Syrians planned to force the Israelis into the widest possible dispersal of its forces on the Golan. The 9th Infantry Division was to drive west, to seize a line of hills south of Kuneitra and cut the Israelis' lines of communication. This was to be the preliminary to the concentration of an overwhelming mass of men, machines and firepower at two critical points where the Syrians would cut through the defences before the Israeli mobilisation system could affect the battle.

In the north, the 7th Infantry Division was to launch holding actions all along its line and invest Wasset. Simultaneously, the Moroccan brigade, which was composed of trained mountain troops, was to operate on the foothills of Mount Hermon and pose a threat to Masada and Banias. Both formations were given limited objectives and orders not to advance further without orders from the Syrian High Command. In the south the penetration was to be made near Rafid by the 5th Infantry Division. The aim was to achieve a double envelopment of the greater part of the forces on Israel's northern front. Thereafter, the 7th Infantry Division was to drive west towards the Upper Jordan through El Rom and Wasset to the northern Jordan crossings while the 5th Infantry Division advanced on a parallel course towards the Arik Bridge, at the northern end of the Sea of Galilee. The plan was for both divisions to advance in two echelons, the breakthrough being exploited by the second echelon. In the event of a breakthrough, elements of 7th Infantry were to combine with the right wing brigade of 9th Infantry to encircle IDF forces in the area of Kuneitra.

Once the 5th Infantry Division had breached the Israeli defences southwest of Rafid, the way would be open for an advance by the 1st Armoured Division up the TAP line from south to north, the mirror image

With vehicle recognition charts above his head, an Israeli soldier observes deep into Syrian territory from his OP high above the Golan Heights on Mount Hermon. Known as 'The Eyes of Israel', its capture by Syrian Commandos on the opening day of the war was a disaster for the Israelis and its recapture became a vital strategic objective before the UN Security Council imposed a ceasefire.

of the Israeli operation in 1967. The 3rd Armoured Division was to be held in reserve to follow on the heels of 1st Armoured Division, a striking example of the concentration of force. Once the breakthrough was achieved, there was to be a maximum effort by the Syrian airborne and armoured forces to seize the Jordan bridges. Heliborne troops were tasked with seizing the Arik and Benot Ya'akov bridges while the two armoured divisions, operating on separate axes – one down the Kuneitra–Benot Ya'akov road, the other down the Hushniyah–Yehudia–Arik Bridge road – would race to link up with the airborne troops on the bridges to block the approach of the IDF reserve divisions.

Critical to the initial Syrian assault was a daring commando attack, at the northern end of the front, against the IDF's electronic intelligence base on Mount Hermon. In addition to its symbolic importance as 'The Eyes of Israel', the base monitored all Syrian air and ground traffic. The base was manned by some 40 intelligence and technical personnel and only 14 infantrymen. The task of taking the post was given to Syria's elite 82nd Parachute Battalion and Special Forces.

When the overall shape of Operation Badr had been hammered out, the focus had necessarily been on its initial stage – the crossing of the Canal by the Egyptians (and the deliberate consolidation of their position on the east bank while pressure was applied to the superpowers) and the breakthrough by the Syrians on the Golan. Enormous care was devoted to the planning of these moves as the preliminaries to the opening of an equally intense diplomatic campaign. Nevertheless, both the Egyptians and Syrians had given some, although less detailed, thought to the second phase of operations. The Syrians had examined crossing the Jordan into eastern Galilee, but the thrust of all their planning with the Egyptians in 1973 had convinced them that a UN ceasefire would be imposed before this extended operation could be launched. The Syrians also had a healthy respect for the IAF and, like the Egyptian high command, were most reluctant to push out beyond their SAM umbrella. The recovery of all or most of the Golan would be reward enough for their endeavour. Syrian intelligence had correctly estimated that the Israelis had less than 200 tanks on the Golan to pit against a total of 1,300. This seemed a very safe margin when military doctrine demands that an attacking force outnumbers its opponent by a ratio of three to one.

# CHRONOLOGY

## 1967

**10 June** Six Day War ends with the capture of the Golan Heights by the IDF and humiliation of Syrian armed forces.

**11 June** The 45th Armoured Brigade (from April 1969 the 188th) or Barak Brigade deploys to defend the Golan Heights area.

**29 August** Arab leaders meet in Khartoum and declare 'Three Noes' – no peace with Israel; no recognition of Israel; no negotiations with Israel.

## 1971

**May** Egyptian armed forces begin planning for war.

**August** Syria breaks off diplomatic relations with Jordan.

## 1972

**24 October** Sadat informs Army High Council of coming war.

## 1973

**21 January** Plans are co-ordinated for combined offensive against Israel.

**3 May** President Assad of Syria visits Moscow and acquires massive new shipments of Soviet weapons including the most modern air defence system.

**7 May** Following major Egyptian manoeuvres along Canal, Israel orders partial mobilisation at great economic expense.

**6 June** Syrian Defence Minister General Tlas arrives in Cairo with a large military delegation to finalise plans for war.

**13 September** Syrian and Israeli combat planes clash over Lebanon with 13 Syrian aircraft destroyed.

**24 September** Using the air battle as a pretext, Syria moves large forces to the disengagement line on the Golan Heights.

**26 September** Yitzhak Rabin, Israel's ambassador to the USA declares; 'There never was a period in which Israel's security situation seemed as good as now.' The 77th OZ Battalion of the 7th Armoured Brigade is ordered to deploy to the Golan Heights in support of the Barak Brigade as a counter-attack force.

**4–5 October** The remainder of the 7th Armoured Brigade deploys to the Golan.

**Saturday 6 October, 1400hrs** War begins on the Day of Atonement (Yom Kippur 5743) when Egyptian and Syrian forces launch co-ordinated offensives across the Suez Canal and on the Golan Heights. Heavy tank battles take place throughout the night as Syrian forces breach the Israeli defences along the Purple Line.

**Sunday 7 October** Syria resumes the offensive with the 1st and 3rd Armoured Divisions launching major attacks in the southern and northern sectors respectively. IAF attacks Syrian armour concentrations and conducts first missions against SA-2 and SA-3 sites.

**Monday 8 October** Heavy fighting continues throughout the day including attacks by the Assad Republican Guard equipped with T-62 tanks. Despite reaching a point overlooking the Sea of Galilee, the Syrians halt their offensive after losing some 600 tanks. IAF mounts first raids against Syrian airbases as well as radar installations and SAM sites.

**Tuesday 9 October** The Syrians launch yet another ferocious assault at 0800hrs together with commando air assaults behind the Israeli lines. In the northern sector the 7th Armoured Brigade is almost overrun. Israeli reserve formations counter-attack on a broad front supported by air power in the southern sector where the Barak Brigade is almost totally destroyed. Syrian forces halt and a tactical withdrawal begins.

**Wednesday 10 October** The IDF continues mopping up operations of the Syrian forces remaining inside the Purple Line. IAF attacks economic targets such as oil refineries and power stations.

**Thursday 11 October** The IDF mounts its major counter-offensive in the northern sector of the Golan Heights on a narrow front towards Damascus with *Ugdas* Raful and Laner. *Ugda* Musa conducts a holding action on the southern sector of the Golan Heights.

**Friday 12 October** Israeli offensive reaches deep into Syria. *Ugda* Laner springs a trap for the 3rd Iraqi Armoured Division with 80 Iraqi tanks destroyed for no Israeli loss.

**Saturday 13 October** After a costly and abortive tank attack against Tel Shams on the previous day, a battalion of paratroopers captures the feature suffering just four wounded.

**15**

**Sunday 14 October** IDF halts offensive and consolidates its positions in its salient inside Syria within artillery range of Damascus.

**Monday 15 October** IAF attacks Iraqi reinforcements arriving in Syria. The Israelis switch priority of supplies and airpower to the Sinai Desert against the Egyptians.

**Tuesday 16 October** Jordanian 40th Armoured Brigade mounts an unsupported attack against *Ugda* Laner.

**Wednesday 17 October** *Ugda* Musa replaces *Ugda* Laner inside the salient with all Israeli forces consolidating their positions as long-range artillery bombards the outskirts of Damascus.

**Thursday 18 October** For the next four days, Syrian, Iraqi and Jordanian forces mount unco-ordinated and generally ineffective attacks against Israeli positions.

**Saturday 20 October** The most effective of these attacks occurs in a seven-hour battle with the Arab forces losing some 120 tanks.

**Monday 22 October** A combined operation by heliborne paratroopers and Golani infantrymen recaptures Mount Hermon. UN ceasefire comes into effect at 1852hrs that night.

**Tuesday 23 October** Second ceasefire comes into effect but violations continue on both the northern and southern fronts.

**Wednesday 24 October** The Soviet Union threatens to send troops to support the Arabs. Second ceasefire brings hostilities to a halt with Israeli forces around 100km from Cairo and within artillery range of Damascus.

**October 1973–May 1974** Syrians continue hostilities with war of attrition against Israeli salient.

# 1974

**June** Following the Israeli/Syrian Disengagement Agreement, Israeli forces withdraw to the 1967 ceasefire line.

**July** Disengagement of Israeli and Arab forces is completed under UN auspices with buffer zone created between the Israelis and Syrians.

# 1981

**14 December** Israel formally annexes the Golan Heights.

# OPPOSING ARMIES

## SYRIAN FORCES

I dentified Syrian formations on the Golan front were, from north to south, as follows: in the foothills of Mount Hermon was a Moroccan brigade; to the north of the Kuneitra–Damascus road was the 7th Infantry Division with an attached armoured brigade; south of the road and with a front extending from Kuneitra to just north of Rafid was the 9th Infantry Division, also with an attached armoured brigade; south and east of Rafid and north of the Yarmouk Valley was the 5th Infantry Division with a reinforced tank component and an attached armoured brigade. Behind these formations was a second echelon: 3rd Armoured Division deployed between Katana, its permanent camp, and Sasa; 1st Armoured Division south and west of its permanent base of Kiswe.

A Syrian infantry division contained the following main combat elements: one infantry brigade, two mechanised infantry brigades, and one armoured brigade. The infantry and mechanised infantry brigades had three infantry battalions, a battalion of 40 tanks (T-54s or T-55s) and a field artillery battalion. The armoured brigades fielded three 40-tank battalions. Other components of a Syrian infantry division included regiments of field and anti-aircraft artillery, a reconnaissance battalion and a chemical warfare company. Syrian brigades of all types had a troop of four PT-76 reconnaissance tanks per company and another for each battalion and brigade HQ.

The Syrian Army also employed the eight-wheeled BTR-60 APC in significant numbers. This model is the BTR-60PB with an enclosed turret housing a 14.5mm KPVT heavy machine-gun and a co-axial 7.62mm PKT.

These units gave the division a strength on paper of some 10,000 men, 200 tanks, 72 artillery pieces and approximately the same number of anti-aircraft guns and SAMs. The real figures at the beginning of October were, however, markedly different. Only the 5th Infantry Division had its full complement of armoured and mechanised vehicles; the 7th Infantry Division had only 80 per cent of its tanks and APCs and in the case of 9th Infantry Division the figure dipped to 50 per cent. Nevertheless, the designation 'infantry' is misleading, as these Syrian infantry divisions were essentially mechanised formations.

However, both Syrian armoured divisions, 3rd and 1st, were at full strength. Each of their two armoured brigades contained 120 tanks and, with a mechanised infantry brigade, they could put more than 250 tanks into the field with the same supporting units as an infantry division. For the attack on the Golan, Syrian forces numbered some 60,000 men, 1,400 tanks and 800 guns.

# ORDER OF BATTLE

## SYRIAN ARMY, OCTOBER 1973 [1]

### Cabinet & GHQ
Hafaz al Assad, President of Syria
Major General Mustafa Tlas, Minister of Defence
Major General Youssef Chakkour, Chief of Staff
Major General Abdul Razzaq Dardary, Chief of Operations
Major General Jibrael Bitar, Director of Intelligence
*GHQ Forces*
Assad Republican Guard Armoured Brigade
30th Infantry Brigade
90th Infantry Brigade
62nd Independent Infantry Brigade
88th Armoured Brigade
141st Armoured Brigade
1st Commando Group
82nd Parachute Battalion
Desert Guard Battalion

*Western Syria*
Latakia – Infantry Brigade
Homs – Infantry Brigade
Aleppo – Infantry Brigade

+ Moroccan Expeditionary Brigade
+ Saudi Arabian 20th Armoured Brigade (King Abdul Aziz Brigade)
+ Two commando brigades of the Palestinian Liberation Army

### 1st Armoured Division – Colonel Tewfiq Juhni
4th Armoured Brigade
91st Armoured Brigade
2nd Mechanised Infantry Brigade
64th Artillery Brigade

### 3rd Armoured Division – Brig Gen Mustafa Sharba
20th Armoured Brigade
65th Armoured Brigade
15th Mechanised Infantry Brigade
13th Artillery Brigade

### 5th Infantry Division – Brigadier General Ali Aslan
12th Infantry Brigade
61st Infantry Brigade
132nd Mechanised Infantry Brigade
50th Artillery Brigade
47th Independent Armoured Brigade (attached)

### 7th Infantry Division – Brigadier General Omar Abrash [2]
68th Infantry Brigade
85th Infantry Brigade
1st Mechanised Infantry Brigade
70th Artillery Brigade
78th Independent Armoured Brigade (attached)

### 9th Infantry Division – Colonel Hassan Tourkmani
52nd Infantry Brigade
53rd Infantry Brigade
43rd Mechanised Infantry Brigade
89th Artillery Brigade
51st Independent Armoured Brigade

### *Iraqi Forces*
### 3rd Armoured Division – Brigadier General Lafta
6th Armoured Brigade
12th Armoured Brigade
8th Mechanised Infantry Brigade
+ Artillery Group

### *Jordanian Forces*
40th Armoured Brigade – Brigadier Haled Hajhouj al Majali

---

**1** Source: *Elusive Victory – The Arab-Israeli Wars 1947–1974* by Colonel Trevor Dupuy, Macdonald and Jane's, London 1978
**2** Killed in action on 8 October 1973. He was replaced by Brigadier General Said Berakdar

The most powerful tank in the Arab armies during the October War was the T-62 with its formidable 115mm main armament and automatic loading system. Although it had been encountered before the October War, the T-62 came as a rude shock to the Israelis as did the tenacity and determination of the Syrian crews who continued to attack despite appalling casualties.

The Syrian Air Force, commanded by Major General Maji Jamil, had over 300 aircraft, including 30 Su-7 and 80 MiG-17 ground-attack aircraft, 200 MiG-21 interceptors and a small number of Il-28 light bombers. However, mindful of the mauling it had received at the hands of the IAF on 13 September, the Syrians, like the Egyptians, integrated the air force with the SAM air defence system for the coming attack. West of Damascus they deployed about 100 SAM batteries and, in addition to divisional AA weapons, some 30 anti-aircraft companies equipped with 160 guns, many of them ZSU-23-4 multi-barrelled, self-propelled anti-aircraft cannon.

# ISRAELI FORCES

Against the formidable Syrian forces assigned to the attack on the Golan Heights, the Israelis deployed just a single under-strength armoured brigade, two infantry battalions and four batteries of self-propelled artillery. The reason for this alarming imbalance was simple – the Israelis did not believe the Syrians would attack without Egyptian co-operation and the Egyptians would not go to war for at least another three years. This was the received wisdom of the Israeli intelligence community and nothing would change this perception. Any Syrian incursion would be met by the full force of the mighty Israeli Air Force that had paved the way for the stunning victory in 1967. By 1973, the air force absorbed 52 per cent of the Israeli defence budget and the other combat arms were being starved of resources accordingly, particularly the infantry and the artillery branches. The infantry were equipped with outmoded personal weapons and the venerable M3 Halftrack remained the principal battlefield transport as the M113 APC [Armoured Personnel Carrier] had been procured in relatively small numbers. Worse still the artillery had only a limited number of modern self-propelled guns such as the M107, M109 and M110. It was the role of the air force to provide fire support to the ground troops and pound the enemy to destruction while the formidable Israeli fighters provided complete air superiority over the battlefield.

Thus the resident garrison on the Golan supported by the overwhelming firepower of the air force was deemed to be sufficient deterrent to invasion

The Israeli Artillery Corps was very much the poor relation of the IDF's various branches prior to the October War as, according to Israeli doctrine, it was the task of the air force to provide the majority of the fire support to the ground troops on the battlefield. As a result, there were too few self-propelled artillery batteries equipped with modern weapons such as this 175mm M-107 gun bombarding Syrian positions.

and more than adequate to counter any limited incursion. If war seemed imminent, the intelligence services would give at least 48 hours notice during which time the well-oiled wheels of mobilisation would be set in motion with reserves arriving at the front as war broke out. Reserve divisions would then be deployed to each of the fronts depending on the situation, be it Northern Command facing Lebanon and Syria; Central Command bordering Jordan and Southern Command in the Sinai against the Egyptians. Such was the theory but the Arabs had devised a counter to all these measures. The stage was set for war.

# ORDER OF BATTLE

## ISRAELI NORTHERN COMMAND, OCTOBER 1973

**Cabinet**

Mrs Golda Meir, Prime Minister
General Moshe Dayan, Minister of Defence

**Israel Defense Forces GHQ**

LtGen David 'Dado' Elazar, Chief of Staff
MajGen Israel 'Talik' Tal, Deputy Chief of Staff
MajGen Eliezer Ze'ira, Chief of Intelligence

**Northern Command**          **Central Command**          **Southern Command**

MajGen Yitzhak 'Haka' Hofi

Ugda *Raful (36th Armoured Division) – BrigGen Rafael 'Raful' Eitan*
188th Armoured Brigade 'Barak' – Col Yitzhak Ben Shoham
7th Armoured Brigade – Col Avigdor 'Yanush' Ben Gal
1st Infantry Brigade 'Golani' – Col Amir Drori
31st Parachute Brigade – Col Elisha Shelem

Ugda *Laner (240th Reserve Armoured Division) – BrigGen Dan Laner*
17th Reserve Armoured Brigade – Col Ran Sarig
679th Reserve Armoured Brigade – Col Uri Orr
+ Elements of the Barak Brigade from 7 October

Ugda *Musa (146th Reserve Armoured Division) – BrigGen Moshe 'Musa' Peled*
4th Reserve Armoured Brigade – Col Ya'akov 'Pepper' Hadar
9th Reserve Armoured Brigade – Col Mordechai Ben Porat
70th Reserve Armoured Brigade – Col Gideon Gordon
205th Reserve Armoured Brigade – Col Ben Yossi Peled

# OPPOSING COMMANDERS

**Major General Mustafa Tlas, was the Syrian Minister of Defence and overall field commander during the October War. His decision to establish his field headquarters midway between Damascus and the frontlines so as to fulfil both his military and political functions was a major blunder. At critical stages of the battle, he ordered his field commanders to break off their operational duties to return to his headquarters, wasting valuable time when resolute decisions were required. Arguably this lack of flexibility in the command structure was to deny the Syrians victory in the October War.**

The fortunes of war are fickle and varied and the outcome of battle is most often dictated by the quality of the most basic component – the soldier. Whether commander or infantryman, the fate of nations can depend on his performance on the battlefield. The war on the Golan was just such an encounter with the survival of the state of Israel at stake. Although few individual actions can be genuinely considered fundamental to the outcome of a battle, there are particular decisions and particular events that can tip the balance. Predominantly it is the judgement of commanders that determines victory or defeat.

## SYRIAN COMMANDERS

Early in 1973, General Ahmed Ismail, the Egyptian War Minister, began to hammer out a common strategy with his opposite number in Syria, **Major General Mustafa Tlas**. Tlas was one of the many politically conscious officers in the Syrian Army and had visited Moscow, Peking and Hanoi. He had written books on guerrilla warfare and the campaigns of the prophet Mohammed. He had also been appointed as the overall field force commander on the Golan. Establishing his headquarters halfway between Damascus and the front line in an attempt to co-ordinate the separate functions of political control and command in the field, Tlas fatally fell between two stools. Because he felt unable to leave his head-quarters to visit his subordinate commanders and take personal stock of the situation, he was obliged to recall them at critical moments when they should have been controlling the tactical battle. It was to have a profound effect on the outcome of the war.

The Syrian Chief of Staff was Major General Youssef Chakkour, an Alawite; the director of operations was Major General Abdul Razzaq Dardary, whose deputy was Brigadier Abdullah Habeisi, a Christian more concerned with military strategy and tactics than political manoeuvring. To many officers in the higher echelons of the Syrian armed forces, a military career was simply a means of political advancement rather than the profession of arms in the defence of the state. There were of course some notable exceptions.

**Brigadier General Omar Abrash**, general officer commanding the Syrian 7th Infantry Division, was a graduate of the US Army Command and General Staff College at Fort Leavenworth. General Abrash led his division from the front and was directing operations at the anti-tank ditch as his forces opened the attack towards Kuneitra. In his path were the Centurions of the 77th Battalion of the 7th Armoured Brigade. Repeatedly, Abrash hurled his tanks at the Israeli positions with desperate gallantry. By the late afternoon of 8 October, the 7th Armoured Brigade

The Israeli Defence Minister, General Moshe Dayan visits troops on the Golan Heights in company with Major General Yitzhak 'Haka' Hofi, the commander of the Northern Front during the October War. Dayan's deeply pessimistic assessment of the fighting on the Golan Heights during the first days of the war led to much despondence in the Israeli cabinet and GHQ but it did lead to the total commitment of the IAF and reinforcements to the Northern Front at the expense of Southern Command in the Sinai.

was on the verge of collapse. At dusk on that fateful Monday evening, Abrash rallied his remaining tanks for one last attack relying on the Syrians' superiority in night-fighting equipment to overwhelm the Israelis. At that critical juncture, Abrash's tank was hit by an APDS round and burst into flames, killing the courageous commander. The attack was fatally postponed until morning, granting the 77th Battalion some vital respite and time for reinforcement. Lacking Abrash's dynamic leadership, the attack was contained after fierce fighting and the Syrian onslaught faltered, never to recover.

# ISRAELI COMMANDERS

In 1973 the Chief of Staff of the IDF was **Lieutenant General David 'Dado' Elazar.** Born in Sarajevo in 1925, he distinguished himself as a member of the *Palmach* during the War of Independence in 1948. He was an infantry brigade commander in the 1956 Sinai campaign, after which he became the commander of the Israeli Armoured Corps from 1957 to 1961. Thereafter he always wore the tankers' black beret and he did much to foster the predominance of the tank within the Israeli Army. In 1962 he was promoted to Major General and four years later took over Northern Command, where he was responsible for the brilliant campaign to capture the Golan Heights during the Six Day War. On 1 January 1972 he became the Chief of Staff of the IDF.

By a quirk of fate, the majority of the top posts within the Israeli Army changed during the months leading up to the October War so the new incumbents were relatively inexperienced; for instance, the GOC of Central Command took up his appointment just six days before the war began. Hours before the outbreak of the October War, the Israeli cabinet ordered the partial mobilisation of the reserves but Elazar on his own authority organised a general mobilisation – it was a critical decision that did much to save the state of Israel. After the war, however, the Agranat Commission found him negligent in failing to read Arab intentions. He resigned as Chief of Staff on 2 April 1974 and the Labour

Brigadier General Rafael 'Raful' Eitan was the commander of the inadequate forces tasked with defending the Golan Heights from Syrian attack. A tenacious character he refused to countenance retreat and handled his ever-diminishing units with adroit skill against overwhelming odds until sufficient reserves arrived on the Golan Heights to rescue the desperate situation.

government of 30 years fell soon afterwards. He died while playing tennis in 1977.

**Major General Yitzhak Hofi** was appointed general officer commanding Northern Command in 1972. Like so many officers in the IDF, he had acquired a nickname and was known as 'Haka'. A quietly spoken, dour man of few words, Hofi exuded an air of firm authority born of many years' experience of border fighting as a paratroop commander. During the autumn and winter of 1972/73, his command fought several bitter 'battle days' when the Syrians crossed the ceasefire line and clashed with Israeli forces. In the second of these 'battle days', the Syrians used Sagger ATGW missiles for the first time in large numbers, destroying several Israeli tanks. Hofi immediately issued his frontline troops with more mortars to counter the Sagger and on the next 'battle day' they proved so effective that the menace was largely neutralised and very few hits were sustained. Hofi also launched a comprehensive overhaul of the military infrastructure of Northern Command, during which hundreds of kilometres of unpaved tracks were created, to speed the deployment of artillery and tanks across the Golan. At intervals along the tracks, tank ammunition (200 rounds per tank on the Golan as of 6 October 1973) was dumped to ease replenishment. The armoured mobilisation centres were also moved closer to the frontline near the Sea of Galilee including Rosh Pina, the Headquarters of Northern Command. Rigorous exercises confirmed that these measures cut mobilisation times by up to half – this would prove crucial after 6 October. Simultaneously, the anti-tank ditch in front of the Purple Line was extended and deepened to slow any Syrian attempt at an armoured breakthrough and channel their tanks into prepared killing grounds. Only days before the war, further minefields were laid along the Purple Line. Hofi's preparations in the months before the war were to play a vital part in the success of Israeli arms. Like his counterpart at Southern Command, Major General Shmuel Gonen, Hofi was to suffer intense pressure in the opening days of the war but, unlike Gonen, 'Haka's' reputation survived the October War intact. Major General Yitzhak Hofi subsequently became the head of Mossad, Israel's Secret Service.

The forces stationed on the Golan were commanded by **Brigadier General Rafael 'Raful' Eitan**. Another taciturn man of stocky build and dark complexion, Eitan was first and foremost a farmer and happiest when tending his animals. After leaving the army in the early 1950s, he returned to farming. During the war of 1956, however, a friend reproached him, saying: 'They are killing Jews and you are milking cows.' Eitan rejoined the army as a paratrooper and gained a reputation as a ferocious fighter. He was considered by many colleagues to be a safe pair of hands but of no great intellect. Eitan was shot in the head during the 1967 war; when he was subsequently promoted many thought it proved that you did not need brains for advancement in the IDF. He subsequently led the reprisal raid that destroyed 13 Arab airliners at Beirut Airport on 28 December 1968. After blowing up the planes, he calmly strolled into the transit lounge bar and ordered drinks for his men. As commander of the 36th Armoured Division or *Ugda* Raful, Eitan was temperamentally suited to the desperate defensive battle fought on the Golan – courageous with keen tactical skill and a refusal to countenance retreat. He remained at his underground bunker headquarters at Nafekh until Syrian tanks were literally at his door. His fellow commanders on the Golan were equally impressive.

As the commander of *Ugda* Musa, the 146th Reserve Armoured Division, Brigadier General Moshe 'Musa' Peled issues orders from his M3 halftrack command vehicle during the counter-attack on the Golan Heights. After the October War, he became the commander of the Israeli Armoured Corps.

**Brigadier General Dan Laner** was an experienced officer whose war record stretched back to World War II. During the Six Day War of 1967, he led the attack that captured the Golan Heights. In February 1973 he was released from active service but in May, fearing the outbreak of war, General Elazar directed him to form and activate a new reserve division as soon as possible. On 6 October he rushed to the Golan Heights and quickly realised the gravity of the situation. Rather than waiting to mobilise his entire formation as instructed, Laner stood on the Benot Ya'akov Bridge acting as a military policeman and directing platoons and companies of tanks up the escarpment as soon as they were formed. It was to prove a vital measure in stemming the Syrian onslaught. That night, Laner suggested to Hofi that he take over responsibility for the southern half of the Golan while Eitan directed operations in the north. Hofi was quick to agree. It was this flexibility in command and control by the field commanders and the stubborn resistance of their men that allowed the Israelis to contain the Syrian onslaught. Laner's *Ugda* subsequently led the major thrust of the Israeli counter-attack back to the Purple Line and into Syria. His appreciation of Iraqi 3rd Armoured Division's intentions and the trap he laid to destroy their offensive were masterly. Brigadier General Dan Laner is generally recognised as being the 'man of the match' in the war on the northern front. After the war, he returned to a well-earned retirement.

An equally formidable leader was **Brigadier General Moshe 'Musa' Peled**. Another farmer by birth, Peled was an outspoken, hard-bitten armour officer who was GOC of the 146th Reserve Armoured Division (*Ugda* Musa) following his appointment as the commandant of the Command and General Staff School of the IDF. Unlike many in the IDF high command, Peled was convinced that war would break out in 1973 and he trained his troops accordingly. Although due to take up a new appointment from 3 October, Peled immediately rejoined his division on Yom Kippur. As he drove to the depot at Ramle, his car was stoned by orthodox Jewish children for travelling on the holiest day of the year. The mobilisation of *Ugda* Musa went to plan but much of its equipment was outdated including old Sherman and petrol-engined Centurion tanks. As a division of the strategic reserve, *Ugda* Musa was originally slated for service in Sinai, but on the second day of the war General Elazar ordered the division to the Golan Heights. Many of its tanks broke down en route for want of tank transporters. Once again a field commander took a decisive executive decision. Peled decided to commit his division along the road south of the Sea of Galilee towards El Al and up the Gamla Rise rather than, as his orders specified, over the Arik Bridge, which was the main line of communication for *Ugda* Laner. His prompt action did much to contain a dangerous Syrian thrust towards the heart of Israel. After heavy fighting in the southern Golan, Peled's division relieved *Ugda* Laner in the closing days of the war and was then transferred to the Southern Front in Sinai. After the October War, Brigadier General 'Musa' Peled became the commander of the Israeli Armoured Corps from 1974 to 1979 and did a fine job rebuilding the *Heyl Shirion* into a modern combined arms force equipped with the indigenously produced Merkava MBT, which incorporated many lessons from the high-intensity combat of the 1973 war.

# THE BATTLE FOR THE GOLAN

I n the summer of 1973, the Soviet training mission moved into high gear as the Syrians struggled to absorb a flood of Russian hardware. One of the most significant additions to the Syrian arsenal was the arrival and installation of an extremely sophisticated air defence system. Soviet advisers and technicians undertook the task of integrating an array of SAMs with a range of altitudes and radar and optical fire-control systems backed by ECM. Soviet advisers also maintained a presence in every Syrian command post and combat formation in the battle zone. In the rear, Soviet technicians assembled combat aircraft shipped in by air and sea including MiG-21s and Su-22s.

At the beginning of August, Egyptian and Syrian planning groups met in Alexandria to analyse the respective degrees of readiness of their armed forces and to assess the situation in Israel. However, the choice of Y-Day (*Yom* meaning Day in both Hebrew and Arabic) was a political decision to be made by Sadat and Assad; they opted for 6 October, when a range of factors operated in favour of Egypt and Syria.

For the Canal crossing, the Egyptians needed moonlight in the first phase of operations to help them establish bridges across the Canal. Later they needed darkness to push men and vehicles over to the east bank. In contrast, the Syrians argued for a daylight advance across the Golan plateau. The Egyptians needed favourable tides and currents in the Canal; the Syrians wanted to avoid the driving rain that usually

Based on the chassis of the PT-76 amphibious tank, the ZSU-23-4 proved to be a highly effective weapon system during the October War and inflicted significant losses on the Israeli Air Force in the early days of the hostilities. Its quadruple 23mm cannons were radar guided and normally fired bursts of 50 rounds a barrel to a combat range of 2,500m (8,200ft).

enveloped the Golan plateau in November and the snow that blanketed Mount Hermon in December.

As 6 October, the tenth day of Ramadan, was the traditional anniversary of the battle of Badr won by the prophet Mohammed in AD626, the military aspect of Operation Spark was assigned the codename Badr by the Egyptians and Syrians. S-Hour (*Sifr* is Arabic for zero) remained a matter of debate. The Egyptians wanted an hour in the late afternoon, the Syrians one early in the morning; both wanted the sun behind them shining in the eyes of the Israelis. It was not until 2 October in Damascus that Egypt's General Ismail secured a compromise from Assad. S-hour was set at 1400 hours.

On 6 September, Ismail issued a Federal General Directive, placing both Egyptian and Syrian armed forces on a 'five-day alert' from 1 October. A week later, a fierce air battle took place over Tartous in Syria after Syrian MiG-21s scrambled to intercept Israeli Air Force (IAF) F-4 Phantoms and Mirage IIICs photographing arms deliveries by Soviet ships. In the air battle that followed, the IAF claimed 13 Syrian aircraft shot down while the Syrians admitted to eight and claimed five kills. There were in fact no IDF losses. During the engagement the Syrians were eager to unleash their SAMs, but the Soviet advisers refused to hand over the vital fuses they had retained; a wise decision as it turned out.

The Syrians' well-advertised plans to meet further aggression provided a useful cover for their concentration on the Golan. They also urged the Egyptians to advance the date of Operation Badr, but General Ismail insisted that the original timetable be adhered to. The deception plan was maintained to the last minute. On the southern front, the Egyptians concentrated under the cover of Exercise 'Tahir 73' (Liberation 73), the annual autumn manoeuvres, while continuing the dialogue with American and UN officials over a wide range of peace proposals. The Syrians also joined them in exploiting the news media to sow stories of 'business as usual'. For example, on 4 October Damascus Radio announced that Assad would begin a nine-day tour of Syria's eastern provinces on 10 October. Meanwhile newspapers in both countries reported a deep political rift between Assad and Sadat.

In contrast to their indifferent performance during the Six Day War, most Syrian soldiers fought with tenacity and dogged determination during the opening days of the October War, although their training did not allow great tactical flexibility on the battlefield. Syrian marksmen and RPG teams repeatedly infiltrated the Israeli lines at night and exacted a fearful toll of Israeli tank commanders and vehicles. Once forced onto the defensive, the Syrian command structure suffered badly with the wounded often abandoned on the battlefield. Nevertheless, when the Israelis invaded Syria itself, the Syrians put up stout resistance. The Israeli advance faltered with the IDF unwilling to be drawn into a battle of attrition when it was more important to transfer formations to the Sinai Front.

Both Sadat and Assad also needed to 'deceive' their own troops, all the way up to senior field and staff officers. Very few of their soldiers knew that they were going to war until a few minutes before the offensive was actually launched. The highest-ranking Egyptian to fall into Israeli hands during the war, a colonel, told his interrogators that the first he heard of it was just after 1330hrs on 6 October when his commanding officer, a lieutenant general, rose from his prayers to inform his subordinate that war was about to begin – an announcement followed immediately by a flight of jets roaring overhead to bomb targets in Sinai.

Members of the Syrian *Fedayeen* guerrillas, the *Saiqua*, played a significant role in the deception plan to which Assad gave only reluctant consent. On 28 September, two *Saiqua* gunmen hijacked a train in Austria and took several Jewish passengers hostage. The resolution of this crisis proved to be a considerable distraction for the Israeli cabinet in the days leading up to the opening of Operation Badr. It also provided another cover for the Egyptian and Syrian mobilisations, as it could be plausibly argued that retaliatory measures by the IDF were now anticipated after the outrage in Austria.

On 3 October, the Soviet Union launched COSMOS-596, the first of a series of reconnaissance satellites, into orbit over the Middle East to cover Israel's northern and southern fronts. The Americans had launched a satellite performing the same function on 27 September. On the day of the Soviet satellite launch the Soviet Union began to withdraw Soviet personnel from Egypt, followed two days later by their personnel in Syria. On the night of 4 October, Syrian armour on the Golan moved from a defensive to an offensive posture.

By September 1973 it was clear to the Israelis that a massive Syrian build-up was gathering momentum east of the Purple Line. Initially, Israeli intelligence chose to interpret this as no more than evidence of the training exercises that had taken place in previous years. However, from 20 September IAF reconnaissance photographs revealed that there were

**With a crew of three comprising commander, gunner and driver as well as an infantry section of eight soldiers, the BMP-1 Infantry Fighting Vehicle saw its combat debut during the October War. Armed with a 73mm smoothbore gun and a Sagger ATGW, the vehicle is fully amphibious and, for the first time, allowed the infantry in the back to fire their weapons from under armour, albeit in extremely cramped conditions. In Syrian hands, the BMP-1 did not prove very effective and according to Israeli sources not a single BMP-1 IFV managed to cross the Purple Line.**

One of the critical decisions that saved the Golan Heights from capture by the Syrians was the deployment of the regular 7th Armoured Brigade to Northern Command. At its base around Beersheba it had trained for desert warfare in the Sinai and as such was unfamiliar with the terrain on the Golan Heights. The 77th Battalion was the first of its units to be moved to the Golan, where it arrived on 4 October. It was to act as a reserve to the 188th Barak Brigade, under whose command it was placed. It had left its vehicles in the south and requisitioned 22 replacements from Northern Command war stocks.

now three Syrian infantry divisions, with attached tank brigades, in their frontline and more mechanised and infantry units in the second line. An IDF intelligence estimate placed Syrian strength on the Golan at around 670 tanks and 100 batteries of artillery. Opposing this concentration on the other side of the Purple Line was one under-strength armoured brigade, the 188th Barak Armoured Brigade, and two infantry battalions.

The Israeli GOC Northern Command, Major General Yitzhak Hofi, was concerned by the Syrian concentration. At a meeting of the Israeli General Staff held on 24 September, Hofi pointed out that if it continued the Syrian build-up would be unprecedented in scale. The Syrians could attack without warning and with overwhelming force. In contrast to the Sinai, space could not be traded for time. Equally worrying was the introduction into the equation of the SAM batteries. The Chief of Staff, Lieutenant General David Elazar, echoed Hofi's concern. By contrast, the head of Israeli military intelligence, Major General Eliezer Ze'ira, was unruffled by the shape events were taking on Israel's Northern Front.

Ze'ira, who had only been in his post since the spring of 1973, subscribed to what the Israelis termed 'The Concept', a theory which ran as follows: Syria would only attack Israel in concert with Egypt; Egypt would not attack Israel until its air force had recovered from the catastrophe of 1967, a process that would take at least another five years; therefore there would be no war in 1973.

The Israeli Minister of Defence, Moshe Dayan, shared Ze'ira's optimism. Nevertheless, Dayan anticipated that the Syrians might respond to the air battle of 13 September and, with this in mind, on 26 September placed the IDF on alert on both the Northern and Southern fronts, although this did not involve mobilisation but simply placed Israel's active units on a war footing. On that day Dayan accompanied LtGen Elazar on a visit to Northern Command, during which he inspected a number of frontline positions. Hofi repeated his warnings as they viewed the concentration, which the Syrians were making only the most perfunctory efforts to conceal. Hofi drew Dayan's attention to the fact that in the Tel

The 115mm smoothbore main armament of Syrian T-62s was able to penetrate all Israeli tanks at normal combat ranges with its fin-stabilised armour-piercing ammunition. Over 400 T-62s equipped the elite Assad Independent Armoured Brigade. Many were captured intact by the Israelis and converted for their own use. It was common practice for Syrian crews to cover the external fuel tanks of their Soviet designed tanks with sandbags in an effort to make them less vulnerable in battle.

Kudne sector, on the Barak Brigade's southern front, there was a high concentration of field artillery, a significant indication of Syria's intention to launch an attack

On the advice of Generals Eitan and Hofi, Dayan then made two vital decisions. First he ordered that the single under-strength Barak Armoured Brigade garrisoning the Golan be reinforced by the 77th Battalion of the elite 7th Armoured Brigade, which was then stationed around Beersheba in southern Israel. The 7th Brigade had been formed in 1948 as the first armoured unit in the IDF and had spearheaded the Israeli thrusts in the Sinai in 1956 and 1967. Eventually, the entire 7th Armoured Brigade was mobilised for service on the Golan. To speed the transfer, the General Staff ordered the brigade commander, Colonel Avigdor 'Yanush' Ben Gal, to leave his own tanks at his training camp and take over tanks and heavy equipment from Northern Command's reserves. Dayan also sent artillery reinforcements north with 7th Armoured Brigade, which concentrated around the divisional headquarters at Nafekh.

By 2 October, Israeli intelligence was reporting an inexorable increase in Syrian strength immediately behind their frontline to 800 tanks and over 120 batteries of artillery. Three days later, on 5 October, the figures had risen again to 900 tanks and 140 artillery batteries. Northern Command intelligence also noted that the Syrian second line of defence was unoccupied, again prompting the conclusion that the Syrians were readying themselves for an attack. Meanwhile, the system designed to cope with the earlier flare-ups on the border swung into action. Leave was cancelled on the Golan and an emergency stand-to was implemented. The machinery of mobilisation was checked and work redoubled on laying more minefields along the frontline.

On 5 October, Brigadier General Rafael Eitan, as commander of the 36th Division, was given permission by Hofi to move the entire 7th Brigade to the Golan Heights. It was to be concentrated as a reserve near Nafekh, poised to counter-attack either north or south of Rafid. Hofi's staff believed that if the Syrians attacked, they would make their main effort in the centre along the Damascus–Kuneitra Road, enveloping Kuneitra from the north

Tank crewmen of the 7th Armoured Brigade dismount from their Centurions armed with Uzi sub-machine guns. Originally the brigade was trained for deployment to the Sinai Desert but its brilliant commander, Colonel Avigdor 'Yanush' Ben Gal had a premonition about the Golan Heights and ordered his battalion and company commanders to tour the frontlines behind the Purple Line in the weeks and days before the October War. It was a fateful decision which allowed the 7th Armoured Brigade to conduct arguably the greatest defensive battle in the annals of armoured warfare, notwithstanding the gallant stand of the 188th Barak Brigade.

and racing on to seize the Benot Ya'akov Bridge over the Jordan River. In contrast, Eitan was anxious about a Syrian thrust south of Kuneitra over ground more favourable to armour.

It was the eve of Yom Kippur, the holiest of all days in Judaism. The IDF was now on the highest state of alert – 'Gimel–C' – for the standing army. The advanced headquarters of Northern Command was moved to the Golan and reserve units were ordered to be ready for mobilisation at a moment's notice. Plans for the evacuation of civilians were readied. Artillery commanders were instructed to prepare targets and firing tables. After intelligence briefing, Colonel Ben Shoham and the senior officers of the Barak Brigade met in an all-night conference in which they reviewed the situation running south from Kuneitra to the Jordanian frontier. Meanwhile, the commander of the 7th Armoured Brigade, Colonel Ben Gal, accompanied his officers on a 'familiarisation' trek over the northern sector of the frontline from the shoulder of Mount Hermon to Kuneitra. The two Israeli brigades on the Golan together fielded a total of 177 Centurion tanks.

On the night of 5 October, a huge weight of traffic struggled towards the Northern Front as personnel, vehicles and ammunition moved to the mobilisation centres. As dawn broke on the 6th all seemed deceptively quiet. Northern Command's brigade commanders were summoned to an urgent meeting at Major General Hofi's headquarters to be informed of an imminent Syrian attack. Although all frontline units were in the highest state of alert it was, nevertheless, Yom Kippur and most soldiers were observing their devotions inside their bunkers, in their tank depots and at their machine-gun posts in the *Mutzavim*. Behind the steel doors of the observation post on Mount Hermon, now firmly locked, services were being held. Hofi informed his subordinates that a Syrian attack was expected at 1800 hours. It was not, however, thought this would be the preliminary to all-out war.

## THE SYRIAN OFFENSIVE

Throughout the initial battles, the Syrians brought a massive volume of artillery fire down on Israeli positions and important features such as crossroads. Many Centurions were damaged by artillery fire, with optical devices and radio antennae proving particularly vulnerable, rendering the tanks blind and without communications. Only one Centurion was completely destroyed by artillery, having been struck by a large-calibre howitzer shell while direct fire anti-tank weapons hit many others.

At 1345hrs spotters on Mount Hermon saw the Syrians remove the camouflage nets from the artillery pieces facing the Purple Line. Ten minutes later shells began to rain down upon Israeli positions along the entire length of the front. In the sectors chosen for the principal and subsidiary breakthroughs, on either side of Rafid and near Kuneitra, the Syrians had achieved a density of between 50 and 80 guns per kilometre, about half the concentration prescribed by strict Soviet doctrine but punishing nevertheless. The bombardment, delivered by artillery pieces ranging from 85 to 203mm calibre, had a numbing effect on the Israelis, sand-blasting the paint from tank hulls, cutting aerials and damaging optics. The bombardment, which lasted 50 minutes, was timed to coincide with the Egyptian crossing of the Suez Canal and was accompanied by air strikes against Israeli command centres and defensive positions.

At Nafekh, senior IDF commanders were attending an orders meeting at Eitan's HQ when it came under attack by Syrian fighter-bombers. As the officers gathered, they heard the roar of approaching aircraft immediately followed by a strafing and bombing attack. To the cacophony was added the crump of shells from Syrian artillery. This signalled the end of the orders group as battalion commanders hurried back to their units and Ben Gal hastily moved his brigade advanced headquarters out of the camp while the bombardment continued.

As Ben Gal's commanders returned to their units, their forward radio links confirmed that their deputies had already activated the IDF's contingency plans and the Centurions were lumbering towards their firing ramps to engage the dense columns of Syrian tanks and APCs that from 1500hrs were swarming towards the ceasefire line. Up to the moment when their engines roared into life, the crews of the Syrian armour had been receiving last-minute instructions from their Soviet advisers. Now the implementation of Operation Badr was in their hands.

**MAJOR SHUMEL ASKAROV, 53RD BATTALION, 188TH BARAK BRIGADE, DEFENDING *MUTZAV* 111 ON THE PURPLE LINE, EVENING, SATURDAY 6 OCTOBER 1973** (pages 32–33)
At just 24 years of age, Major Shumel Askarov was the youngest deputy battalion commander in the Israeli Army. On the morning of 6 October, Askarov insisted on using his *Sho't* Upgraded Centurion to tour his command. At 1356hrs the peace and quiet of Yom Kippur was shattered by a massive Syrian artillery barrage and the exploding bombs of Syrian MiGs (1). Askarov immediately leapt into his tank at the Hushniyah base and drove eastwards towards the Purple Line summoning other tanks of the battalion to follow him. Once at the Purple Line, his *Sho't* (2) and a companion Centurion (3) mounted the tank firing ramps of *Mutzav 111* overlooking Kudne. Askarov's vehicle bears the insignia of the 188th Barak Armoured Brigade on the rear hull (4) although this was not normally carried in combat for security reasons. The infantry strongpoint was defended by a platoon from the 50th Paratroop Battalion under the command of Sergeant Yoram Krivine. The hillock on which *Mutzav 111* was situated offered a clear view far across the 1967 demarcation line. The Syrian bombardment had been under way for almost an hour when clouds of dust were clearly seen approaching from the east. Askarov had chosen the crew for his *Sho't* carefully and it included the finest tank gunner in the Barak Brigade, Yitzhak Hemo from the kibbutz at Kiryat Shmona. As his kibbutz was only a matter of miles behind the frontline, Hemo was fighting for his home and family. Within the first five hours of battle, Askarov and his crew destroyed 35 tanks and APCs

including three of the vital MT-55/MTU-120 bridgelayers (5) that were trying to span the anti-tank ditch to their front. Throughout the late afternoon, the tanks of the Syrian 5th Infantry Division closed on *Mutzav* 111. Around 1900hrs Hemo destroyed a tank at a range of just 50m and Askarov then swung the turret to engage a target just 30m to their right. Both gunners fired at the same moment and both tanks were hit. Askarov was blown out of the turret and fell to the ground with wounds to the face and throat. He was rescued by the paratroopers inside the bunker (6) and evacuated to Safed hospital where he was operated on and told that he would remain in hospital for at least two weeks. Early on Monday morning, he discharged himself and returned to the desperate fighting on the Golan Heights, although he could not speak above a hoarse whisper. He rallied the remnants of the Barak Brigade and together with Colonel Yosi Ben Hannan, who had rushed back to Israel from his honeymoon in Nepal, Askarov scraped together some 13 battle-damaged tanks. This small force rushed to the front and arrived at a critical juncture when the hard-pressed remnants of the 7th Armoured Brigade were just about to be overrun. Both Ben Hanan and Askarov were wounded in the ensuing battle; the latter critically when a Kalashnikov round struck him in the head. Askarov was taken to the Rambam Hospital in Haifa where he was examined by four neurosurgeons. Three of them declared him beyond hope but the fourth surgeon, Yitzhak Shechter, persevered and performed an eight-hour operation that saved Askarov's life. Askarov was awarded the Medal of Gallantry, Israel's second highest decoration. (Howard Gerrard)

Three Syrian divisions – 7th, 9th and 5th – moved forward behind a creeping barrage, bursting across the ceasefire line at pre-selected points to bypass the UN observation posts. The majority of the UN observer posts on the ceasefire line held out for the duration of the war; four were evacuated, three from the Israeli side and one from the Syrian. The observer officers in the posts on the Israeli side were able to maintain contact with UN headquarters in Jerusalem. One of these officers later likened the initial phase of the Syrian advance to a 'parade-ground demonstration'.

This was the fruit of months of careful preparation during which the Syrian tankers had honed tactics based on wave after wave of assaulting tanks rolling forward regardless of casualties and the progress, or lack of it, made by the wave in front. The assaults by the 7th and 5th Infantry Divisions were spearheaded by two slow-moving parallel columns of Armoured Fighting Vehicles (AFVs) intermingled with command and support vehicles as well as towed and tracked anti-tank and anti-aircraft guns. In the vanguard were tanks designed to breach the minefields with rollers in front of their tracks. SU-100 SP guns, based on the T-34 chassis, were also in the vanguard, along with infantry armed with Saggers and RPG-7 rocket-propelled grenades and riding in APCs.

The 5th Infantry Division rumbled forward in good order, although its armour was soon bunched together in an unwieldy mass. The columns of 7th and 9th Infantry Divisions respectively advancing north and south of Kuneitra, fell into confusion from the outset. The bridging tanks needed to cross the Israeli anti-tank ditches were stuck at the rear as road discipline disintegrated under the overwhelming pressure to get to grips with the Israelis.

The Israeli tank crews were ready and waiting. Firing from their ramps and trained to a high standard in long-range gunnery, they concentrated on the gaps that the Syrians had made in the minefields in the Israeli defences. They paid particular attention to the Syrian engineering equipment with accurate APDS fire aimed at the mine-clearing and bridge-laying tanks. One by one they were picked off at ranges of 2,000m

A PT-55 with mine-roller attachment moves along the road near UN Patrol Base 44 and Tel El Merhi after the area was handed back to the Syrians following the Israeli withdrawal on 15 June 1973. These specialised tanks and the MTU-55/MT-55 Bridgelayers were the priority targets for Israeli tank gunners during the first hours of the war to prevent them from breaching the anti-tank obstacles along the Purple Line. (United Nations)

The turret crew of a *Sho't* peer apprehensively at the camera shortly before the war began. This crew is reputedly from the 74th Battalion of the Barak Brigade. After the war, the 7th Armoured Brigade gained much of the credit for saving the Golan Heights from the initial Syrian onslaught but the Barak Brigade was equally worthy of praise as it fought to the last suffering the heaviest casualties of any unit on the Golan with 112 soldiers killed in action.

or more, while behind them a massive traffic jam was building up. In the confusion caused by the accurate Israeli fire, Syrian tanks and APCs were forced off the road while frantic officers tried to restore order. Other tanks were ordered to smash straight through the minefields to clear a path for the bridge-laying armour moving up to deal with the anti-tank ditch. With the heavy losses of combat engineers, the Syrian infantry and tankers who reached the ditch were forced to leave their vehicles and, under heavy Israeli fire, begin to construct causeways with shovels. Eventually some bulldozers were brought up to fill in the ditch.

North of Kuneitra and south of the dominating Mount Hermonit was a ridgeline leading to another hill known to the Israelis as 'Booster', held by some tanks of the Barak Brigade's 74th Battalion, commanded by Lieutenant Colonel Yair Nafshi. The 74th Battalion, one of the two armoured battalions in the Barak Brigade, was strung out in platoons of three tanks to act in close support of the Israeli first line of defence and to deal with any breakthrough between them.

From the vantage point of Booster (known to the Arabs as Tel el Mehafi), Nafshi observed the advancing armoured columns of the Syrian 7th Infantry Division. Through the dust clouds raised by the Syrian artillery and armour, he could make out enemy bulldozer and MTU bridging tanks advancing at the head of the twin columns across a small dish-shaped valley. He ordered his tank crews to concentrate their fire on the bridging tanks. During the afternoon the Israeli tankers, firing at ranges of over 2,000m, accounted for all but two of the Syrian bridging tanks. The two that got away managed to reach the anti-tank ditch opposite Tel Hermonit. Meanwhile the plain below Booster was dotted with the burning hulks of Syrian tanks and APCs. It was the opening phase in a bitter battle for vital ground, which the Israelis were later to call the 'Valley of Tears'.

By the late afternoon of the 6th, Hofi concluded that the Barak Brigade was incapable of holding the entire Golan front against the weight of the Syrian onslaught, particularly south of Kuneitra. Accordingly, he ordered

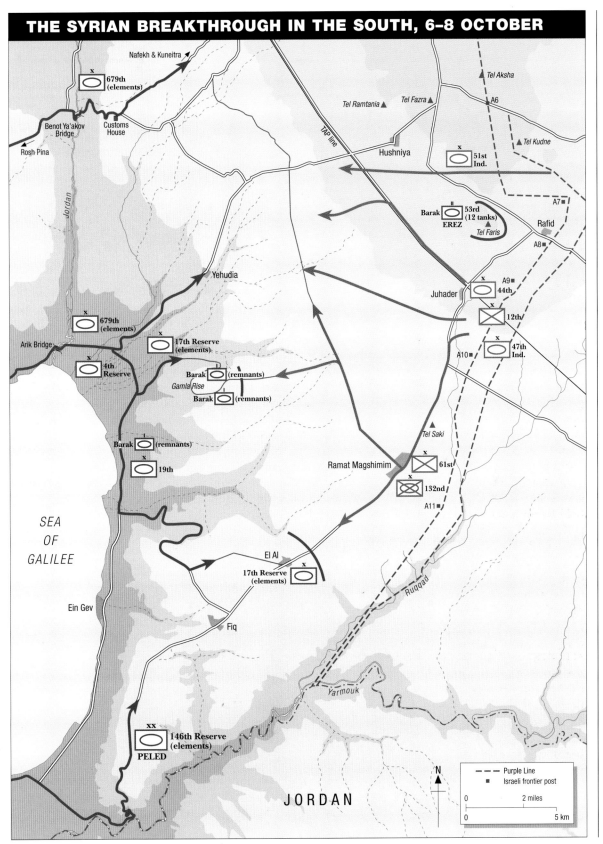

Nafekh & Kuneitra

**x** 679th (elements)

Benot Ya'akov Bridge

Customs House

Rosh Pina

Jordan

TAP line

Tel Aksha

Tel Ramtania

Tel Fazra

A6

Hushniya

Tel Kudne

**x** 51st Ind.

A7

Barak **II** 53rd (12 tanks)

EREZ

Tel Faris

Rafid

A8

**x** 679th (elements)

Arik Bridge

**x** 4th Reserve

**x** 17th Reserve (elements)

Yehudia

Juhader

**x** A9 44th

**xx** 12th

Barak **I** (remnants)

Gamla Rise

Barak (remnants)

**x** A10 47th Ind.

Barak **I** (remnants)

**x** 19th

Tel Saki

Ramat Magshimim

**x** 61st

**x** 132nd

A11

SEA OF GALILEE

Ein Gev

El Al

**x** 17th Reserve (elements)

Ruqqad

Fiq

Yarmouk

**xx** 146th Reserve (elements)

PELED

N

- - - Purple Line
■ Israeli frontier post

0          2 miles

0          5 km

JORDAN

In the open rolling terrain of the Golan Heights, tank crews used every fold in the ground to conceal themselves from enemy observation and direct fire. The rough basalt rock outcrops restricted the movement of tanks to a great degree and forced wheeled vehicles to use the roads and tracks almost exclusively. This left them vulnerable to enemy artillery fire directed by Syrian observers high above the Golan Heights on Mount Hermon, captured by Syrian Special Forces and paratroopers on the first day of the war.

Ben Gal's 7th Brigade to transfer one of its battalions, the 82nd Battalion commanded by Lieutenant Colonel Haim Barak, to the Barak Brigade and simultaneously to take the responsibility for the line north of Kuneitra, assuming command of the Barak Brigade's 74th Battalion, which was already in the thick of the heavy fighting around the Booster feature. One of Ben Gal's battalions, the 71st under the command of Lieutenant Colonel Menachem Ratess, was to be held as a reserve. The 71st Battalion was a composite unit made up of students and instructors from the IDF Armour School that was attached to the 7th Armoured Brigade. Anticipating that he might lose control of this unit, Ben Gal collected a few tanks from each of his battalions to increase the size of his *Sayeret* reconnaissance unit to act as a brigade reserve force of about 20 tanks.

A Centurion *Sho't* of the OZ 77th Battalion manoeuvres to another fire position covered by the gun of a companion vehicle. Commanded by the legendary Lieutenant Colonel Avigdor Kahalani, the 77th Battalion was called the OZ battalion: OZ being the Hebrew word for courage or valour while the number 77 is the numerical equivalent of the Hebrew letters of OZ. The other battalions within the 7th Armoured Brigade were the 71st Armoured Battalion under the command of Lieutenant Colonel Menachem Ratess; the 75th Mechanised Infantry Battalion – Lieutenant Colonel Yoss Eldar and the 82nd Armoured Battalion – Lieutenant Colonel Haim Barak. However, the flexibility of the Israeli command structure allowed battalions to be redeployed to other brigades. In addition ad hoc units were created to carry out particular tasks, acting as a brigade reserve for example.

Meanwhile, Lieutenant Colonel Avigdor Kahalani's companies had moved east, under heavy artillery and air attack, to occupy blocking positions in the Booster sector. His tanks – now reduced to three companies, having lost one to the brigade reconnaissance unit – took up their positions on the ramps overlooking the anti-tank ditch between Hermonit and Booster. Quickly deploying his tanks, designating fire sectors and co-ordinating direct and indirect fire, Kahalani swung his force into action. Battle was joined at odds of almost 15:1. It was to last for over 36 hours.

## The capture of Mount Hermon

In the northernmost sector of the battlefield, Mount Hermon, the IDF suffered a potentially fatal reverse. The Syrians had originally planned to seize the Mount Hermon observation post at S-Hour, but there had been a delay in the briefing and organising of the 500-strong 82nd Parachute Battalion tasked with the operation. It was not until 1400hrs that the Rangers reached the foot of the massif and began to scale it; 45 minutes later they were within 150m of the observation post. Meanwhile, other paratroops had been inserted by helicopter below them to cover the road to Masada. As heavy artillery fire swept the fort and its surrounding defensive positions, the Syrians moved in cautiously, closing with the fort as most of its service personnel sought cover in the deep shelter at its heart. The Rangers had received the most detailed briefing for the operation and each section had a precisely allotted task. The drifting smoke of battle obscured the plain below them.

In their first attempt to rush the position with a frontal attack, the Syrians sustained 50 casualties. They regrouped and began sniping at the Israelis' outer positions while slowly working their way forward. Inside the observation post the non-combatants were frozen with fear and reluctant to come to the aid of the men of the Golani Brigade. At about 1700hrs the Syrians attacked again, coming in from the west with the sun dazzling the

Israeli reinforcements move forward under intense artillery bombardment with knocked-out vehicles strewn beside the road. The view from this M-3 halftrack command vehicle shows the vulnerability of the open-top APC to artillery fire and airburst shells, although many Israeli infantrymen preferred the old M-3 to the cramped interior of the M-113 *Zelda*.

39

**MAJOR QABLAN, SYRIAN 9TH INFANTRY DIVISION,
DIRECTING SPECIALISED AFVS CONFRONTING THE ISRAELI
ANTI-TANK OBSTACLES BEHIND THE PURPLE LINE,
EVENING, 6 OCTOBER 1973** (pages 40–41)

In the organisation of their land forces for the 1973
offensive the Syrians followed Soviet doctrine, deploying
armour en masse. Each of the three attacking infantry
divisions had an integral armoured brigade with 180
T-54/55 tanks. These were backed up by two armoured
divisions, each with 230 of the latest Soviet tank design
then exported – the T-62 with its powerful 115mm main
armament. In addition there were another 400 tanks in
independent brigades giving a grand total of 1,400 tanks.
Syrian military intelligence had determined that the Israelis
had only about 200 tanks on the Golan Heights giving the
Syrians an overall 7:1 advantage; the odds were even
greater at the actual point of attack. However, the nature of
the terrain on the Golan Heights left the Syrians few choices
for the axes of their offensive. Accordingly, the Israelis'
main defensive line was situated on the high ground some
distance behind the 1967 Demarcation Line. At those places
of greatest threat, the Israelis had constructed an anti-tank
ditch (1) to delay the enemy's advance and to channel their
AFVs into prepared 'killing zones'. The actual ditch was
5m wide and 3m deep with the spoil heaped up along the
Syrian side of the ditch to a height of almost 2m. On each
side of the ditch, mines were laid in a belt 3m wide with
anti-tank mines just 1m apart. The dimensions of the ditch
were specifically calculated to thwart the capabilities of
Soviet tank-launched bridging equipment. The advance of

the Syrian 9th Infantry Division has faltered at the edge of
the anti-tank ditch barring the Jasim–Kudne road. The force
commander, Major Qablan (2), calls forward his specialised
armour with a T-55 with KMT mine-roller detonating an
anti-tank mine (3) while an MTU-120 bridgelayer (4) has just
been hit by a *Sho't* of the 188th Barak Brigade on a firing
ramp some 1,500m to the west. Moments later the gallant
Major Qablan's tank was hit by an APDS round and he was
thrown from the turret before his tank exploded in a ball of
fire. Above the battlefield, Israeli Air Force Skyhawks (5) fly
a desperate close support mission to stem the Syrian
assault only to be met by a volley of SAM-6 missiles and
the concentrated fire of radar-guided ZSU-23-4 anti-aircraft
guns (6), which have hit one of the attacking aircraft. UN
observers along the Purple Line recall that the first Israeli
Air Force planes appeared over the Golan Heights just
minutes after war broke out when four Skyhawks flew in
low around Mount Hermon. Before they were able to
engage any Syrian targets, two were blown out of the sky
by SAM-6 missiles. Although temporarily checked at the
anti-tank ditch, the Syrian onslaught continued. As night
fell, the Syrians brought up Caterpillar D-9 Bulldozers and
quickly levelled the ditch. With no night-fighting equipment,
there was little the defending Israeli tanks could do to
stop them as the supporting artillery guns soon ran out of
illuminating rounds. As the sun rose on Sunday 7 October,
the tanks and APCs of the Syrian 43rd Mechanised Infantry
and 51st Armoured Brigades resumed the offensive in
overwhelming force against the dwindling numbers of the
188th Barak Brigade. (Howard Gerrard)

defenders. The Israelis withdrew from the outer defences into the main central position, which was shielded by a high wall. The Rangers, using ropes and grappling hooks, scaled this. Hand-to-hand fighting ensued in which the outnumbered Israelis were overcome. Eleven managed to escape, scrambling down the mountainside and the remainder were taken prisoner.

The Syrians then cleared the underground passages but were unable to break into the main sensor and communications centre, which was protected by its heavy locked steel door. They resorted to stern measures, beating an Israeli prisoner until he unlocked the door. The men inside the communications centre were then shot. On the morning of the 8th an attempt to recapture the Mount Hermon position with a detachment from the Golani Brigade ran into a Syrian ambush and was driven back with losses of 22 killed and 50 wounded. For the remainder of the war the Syrian Rangers, who were troubled only by intermittent air attacks and artillery bombardment, occupied the position. The post's sophisticated Japanese electronic and observation equipment was removed by the Syrians and given to the Soviet Union, much to their delight.

The Syrians were now exerting intense pressure along the entire Israeli line. At about 1700hrs it became clear that the Syrian 5th Infantry Division was threatening to burst through the Rafid Gap towards Juhader. Colonel Ben Shoham hurried to Juhader along the TAP line to direct the battle and re-supply the Barak Brigade's hard-pressed 53rd Mechanised Infantry Battalion, commanded by Lieutenant Colonel Oded Erez. In his half-track, Ben Shoham took with him his operations officer, Major Benny Katzin, while his deputy, Lieutenant Colonel David Yisraeli, remained in Nafekh.

Ben Shoham's advanced headquarters reached Juhader only to come under intense artillery bombardment. The Syrians, who were monitoring Ben Shoham's communications network, kept him pinned down and he was unable to link up with Erez, who was himself surrounded. Ben Shoham now ordered supplies and ammunition to be brought up to re-supply Erez's tanks and APCs as, one by one, they slipped out of their positions to rendezvous with the logistics column. However, before this hazardous manoeuvre could be attempted a lone Syrian tank appeared, probing up the TAP line road.

The Syrian tank, which approached to within a few metres of Ben Shoham's half-track, turned tail and fled. Ben Shoham decided that this was too close for comfort and that he and his ammunition supply convoy should return to Nafekh to organise a counter-attack force. The Syrians now had 150 tanks in the area of Tel Kudne, 60 on the TAP line and a combined total of 140 around frontier posts A9 and A10, respectively north and south of the TAP line.

Unable to return directly to Nafekh, as the Syrians were infiltrating behind him, Ben Shoham had to make a detour by way of the Gamla Rise. The Barak Brigade had been badly battered and by late evening its remaining 15 'runners' faced 450 Syrian tanks. The Syrian infantry's Saggers and RPG-7s had inflicted much damage. The line south of the Juhader road crumbled as the survivors, in groups of twos and threes, concentrated on slowing the Syrian push up the TAP line road, which if successful could turn the entire Israeli position on the Golan.

The Syrian 5th Infantry Division continued to make progress after nightfall. It fanned out into three columns. The northernmost advanced

Three of the decisive commanders of the Golan fighting confer before the war. From left to right, Major General Yitzhak 'Haka' Hofi, Brigadier General Rafael 'Raful' Eitan, commander of the 36th Division and Colonel Yitzhak Ben Shoham, the commander of the 188th Barak Armoured Brigade, who was killed on the second day of the war.

along the TAP line before swinging west to Yehudia and the Arik Bridge, the southern column moved down the road from Rafid towards El Al while the third column peeled away to drive west from Ramat Magshimim. Ben Shoham gave orders for the evacuation of four of his eight frontline strongholds. The remainder were already enveloped and isolated.

The Syrians were well supplied with night-vision equipment for driver, gunner and commander and this soon began to tell. In the Valley of Tears, Kahalani's tankers were now unable to identify targets at long range. Artillery illumination, called in to light up the battlefield, was sporadic – the artillery had only limited supplies of parachute illuminating shells and ammunition was running low. The IAF flew in to drop flares but these did little to dissipate the dark shadows on the floor of the valley. Such illumination as there was came from burning vehicles, and ranges closed to as little as 100m.

Syrian armour rolled forward, using coloured formation signs and flashing blinkers to mark the cleared mine corridors. Kahalani ordered his tank commanders to use their infrared sensitive binoculars to attempt to identify the Syrian formation lamps and infrared 'cat's eyes' winking across the Valley of Tears. The Israeli tank commanders used the Syrian lights to aim their guns, but without proper night-vision equipment, they were still unable to operate effectively at long range.

The fighting in the Valley of Tears was relentless. At 2200hrs the Syrian 7th Infantry Division put in another heavy attack, which was driven off after three hours of close-quarter fighting. The Israelis had also taken losses from the intense Syrian artillery fire. Nevertheless the Syrians were still stuck fast in the Valley of Tears. As dawn came up on 7 October, over 100 Syrian tanks lay damaged or destroyed on the floor of the valley.

At the same time, Ben Shoham received permission from Major General Hofi to take command of all the scattered forces in the southern Golan. South of Juhader, Lieutenant Colonel Oded Erez, commander of the Barak's 53rd Battalion, had called in air support. The four A-4 Skyhawks that flew in to bomb the Syrians were all downed by SAMs, exploding in full view of Erez's men. They were followed by a second flight of four, which lost a further two aircraft to Syrian missiles. Erez declined to call for any more air support. By 0800hrs, another Syrian breakthrough on the TAP line north of the 53rd Battalion removed any hope of their linking up with Ben Shoham and Erez was given permission to withdraw from Juhader and concentrate his force of 12 tanks and move to Tel Faris.

Ten kilometres to the southwest of Juhader, the Syrian 5th Infantry Division was exploiting the breakthrough it had made to Ramat Magshimim. As dawn came up, the Syrians enjoyed a magnificent view of the Sea of Galilee and of the town of Tiberias on its western shore. It seemed that victory was within their grasp. Aware that they were still meeting stubborn resistance to the north in the Valley of Tears while on the southern front the IDF forces appeared to be in disarray, the Syrian High Command now threw its weight behind the success in the south. It directed the 1st Armoured Division to exploit the breakthrough at Rafid and ordered the 15th Mechanised Brigade, 3rd Armoured Division to move through the gap between Rafid and Tel Kudne. The Syrian Army was now deploying some 600 tanks in the southern Golan. All that opposed them was Erez's 12 tanks at Tel Faris, a few isolated units that had been cut off along the ceasefire line and a trickle of reserve units that were now beginning to arrive on the Golan.

Ben Shoham, still cut off from the remnants of his forces in the southern Golan, could see the dust clouds of the advancing Syrian columns. At his immediate disposal were one tank and a halftrack. Under fire from Syrian armour he headed for the Gamla Rise, which overlooks the eastern shore of the Sea of Galilee. On the way he gathered units straggling back to the Buteiha Valley and the Arik Bridge. Ben Shoham drove north past the Arik Bridge on a secondary road on the east bank of the Jordan and on to Nafekh, arriving there at about 0900hrs.

He was soon on the move again, setting out down the TAP line to link with his deputy, Colonel Yisraeli, who was now fighting alongside the redoubtable Lieutenant Zwi 'Zwicka' Greengold. It was at this point in the battle that the leading elements of the 679th Armoured Brigade began to arrive, having been rushed piecemeal to the Golan, and were organised into three-tank platoons, netted into a communications network and then sent down the TAP line route to bolster the Barak Brigade. Another ad hoc formation of six tanks was ordered to advance parallel to the TAP line towards Hushniyah, a ruined relic of the 1967 war dominated by a single bullet-scarred minaret, to counter a strong force of Syrian armour.

At about midday, this unit of six tanks reported that it had encountered a force of some 80 Syrian tanks, advanced elements of Syrian 1st Armoured Division, which had burst through the Rafid Gap and now presented a looming threat to the IDF headquarters at Nafekh. Radio contact with the ad hoc group was lost soon afterwards and within another 30 minutes alarming reports were coming in of Syrian tanks around Tel Abu Hanzir only three kilometres to the east of Nafekh. Immediately Eitan ordered Ben Shoham to withdraw down the TAP line to Nafekh and prepare a line of defence.

Eitan also ordered Ben Shoham's deputy, Lieutenant Colonel David Yisraeli, to cover Ben Shoham as he extricated himself. It was during the course of this fighting that Yisraeli was killed after his own tank ran out

One of the primary Syrian objectives was the main Israeli headquarters on the Golan Heights at Nafekh Camp. In the early afternoon of 7 October, Syrian armour burst into the camp causing General 'Raful' Eitan to move his headquarters staff rapidly northwards leaving some administrative personnel to fight off the Syrian onslaught. These three officers formed themselves into a bazooka team and destroyed several tanks including the one in the background, hit as it mounted a perimeter wall where its engine remained running for the next two days.

of ammunition and was shot up by Syrian armour. Unaware of the fate of his deputy, Ben Shoham continued to transmit orders to Yisraeli as he hurried back to Nafekh. He was barely 200m from the base when he was killed by machine-gun fire from a disabled Syrian tank, as was his operations officer, Major Katzin.

Within an hour of Ben Shoham's death, forward elements of the Syrian 1st Armoured Division attacked Nafekh, precipitating the evacuation of Eitan's advanced headquarters, racing out of the northern gate past blazing vehicles, to establish a new headquarters some five kilometres to the north. Syrian shells set the camp ablaze. Eitan later confessed that he had waited until 'it was no longer a disgrace to clear out; when the Syrian tanks had bypassed the camp on both sides'.

On Nafekh's southern perimeter was Lieutenant Colonel Pinie, deputy commander of the Brigade District, who had been ordered by Eitan to establish anti-tank defences around the camp. Now Syrian tanks were bulldozing their way through the perimeter fence and Pinie's men had fled. Beckoning two infantrymen guarding the southern gate with a bazooka, Pinie ran to some rising ground near the fence. Also with him were his operations and district assistant intelligence officers. For the operations officer, now siting the bazooka, it was a baptism of fire. Pinie acted as his number two while the intelligence officer manned a machine-gun.

A Syrian tank approached to within 200m but with his third shot Pinie's operations officer scored a direct hit on the driver's aperture, forcing the crew to abandon their vehicle while the intelligence officer raked them with machine-gun fire. For two days the tank remained entangled in the fence, its engine still running. Shortly after the tank was abandoned, a series of explosions heralded the simultaneous arrival at Nafekh of two more Syrian tanks and the Israeli 679th Reserve Armoured Brigade, which Eitan had ordered down from the Kuneitra sector to hold the line at Nafekh. The Syrian tanks went up in sheets of flame and Pinie and his men raced to the southeast corner of the camp where a battle between Syrian and Israeli armour had erupted. Taking up position, they destroyed one Syrian tank and missed another with their last shell. As the Syrian tank's turret swung towards Pinie and his men, it was blown apart by a shell fired from the tank commanded by Lieutenant Greengold, who had been fighting continuously for almost 20 hours despite being severely wounded.

The intervention of the 679th Reserve Armoured Brigade, whose men had only hours before been going about their civilian lives, had proved crucial. Pitched into a high-intensity armoured battle, they had beaten off a Syrian advance that threatened to sunder the southern front in the Golan. By nightfall, 679th Reserve Armoured Brigade had cleared the area around Nafekh and blunted another armoured thrust by the Syrian 7th Infantry Division, attacking west from Kuneitra.

For both Israel and Syria, the battle on the Northern Front had become a race against time. The Israelis knew that if they could not hold the Syrians until their reserve formations reached the Golan front, northern Galilee would be crushed by the weight of Syrian armour. The IDF was now so short of ammunition that jeeps were scurrying from one disabled tank to another to collect unused shells. For their part, the Syrians were aware that the thin screen of tanks confronting them east and south of the Arik Bridge was all that stood between them and victory. By the afternoon of 7 October, a Syrian brigade was within 1,200m of El Al and another, on the Yehudia road, was less than 10km from the Sea of Galilee.

However, the Syrians had taken heavy casualties, particularly when they had ventured out beyond their SAM umbrella presenting targets to the IAF. Their tanks clung to the roads and made little or no attempt to camouflage or dig in. By late afternoon on 7 October, the Israelis estimated that they had destroyed some 400 Syrian tanks. Mindful of their defeat in 1967, the entire Syrian Army – from generals to the lowliest soldier – was determined not to retreat under any circumstances save orders from higher command. As a result, on meeting stubborn Israeli opposition, middle-ranking Syrian officers were loath to make any tactical withdrawals, even for the purposes of manoeuvring. They simply tried to batter their way through defences that, had they shown greater flexibility and co-ordination, could have been outflanked rather than out-fought. The IDF developed a grudging respect for Syrian courage, but in the final analysis Syrian tactical shortcomings would hand the initiative back to the Israelis.

The IDF, giving priority to the Northern Front, were now flying up replacement tank crews in helicopters that then returned with the

T-55 tanks and BMP-1 Infantry Fighting Vehicles, probably of the Syrian 46th Armoured Brigade, lie burnt and abandoned along the Purple Line near Rafid, the victims of the deadly accuracy of the 188th Barak Brigade in the first hours of the war. (United Nations)

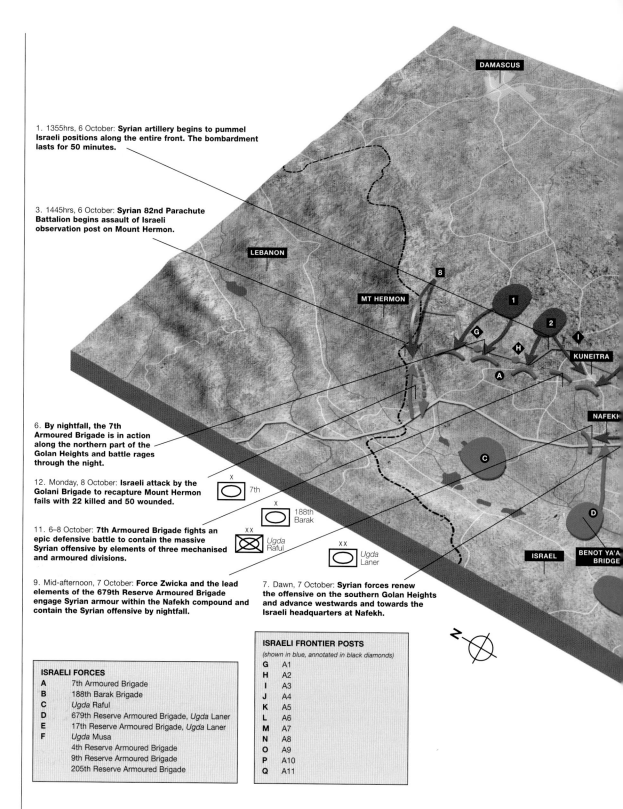

1. 1355hrs, 6 October: **Syrian artillery begins to pummel Israeli positions along the entire front. The bombardment lasts for 50 minutes.**

3. 1445hrs, 6 October: **Syrian 82nd Parachute Battalion begins assault of Israeli observation post on Mount Hermon.**

6. **By nightfall, the 7th Armoured Brigade is in action along the northern part of the Golan Heights and battle rages through the night.**

12. Monday, 8 October: **Israeli attack by the Golani Brigade to recapture Mount Hermon fails with 22 killed and 50 wounded.**

11. 6–8 October: **7th Armoured Brigade fights an epic defensive battle to contain the massive Syrian offensive by elements of three mechanised and armoured divisions.**

9. Mid-afternoon, 7 October: **Force Zwicka and the lead elements of the 679th Reserve Armoured Brigade engage Syrian armour within the Nafekh compound and contain the Syrian offensive by nightfall.**

7. Dawn, 7 October: **Syrian forces renew the offensive on the southern Golan Heights and advance westwards and towards the Israeli headquarters at Nafekh.**

DAMASCUS

LEBANON

MT HERMON

KUNEITRA

NAFEKH

ISRAEL

BENOT YA'A BRIDGE

X
7th

X
188th
Barak

XX
*Ugda*
Raful

XX
*Ugda*
Laner

| ISRAELI FORCES | |
|---|---|
| A | 7th Armoured Brigade |
| B | 188th Barak Brigade |
| C | *Ugda* Raful |
| D | 679th Reserve Armoured Brigade, *Ugda* Laner |
| E | 17th Reserve Armoured Brigade, *Ugda* Laner |
| F | *Ugda* Musa |
| | 4th Reserve Armoured Brigade |
| | 9th Reserve Armoured Brigade |
| | 205th Reserve Armoured Brigade |

| ISRAELI FRONTIER POSTS | |
|---|---|
| *(shown in blue, annotated in black diamonds)* | |
| G | A1 |
| H | A2 |
| I | A3 |
| J | A4 |
| K | A5 |
| L | A6 |
| M | A7 |
| N | A8 |
| O | A9 |
| P | A10 |
| Q | A11 |

# THE SYRIAN OFFENSIVE

6–8 October 1973, viewed from the south-west showing the initial Syrian assault
across the Purple Line and the breakthrough around Rafid and Hushniya.

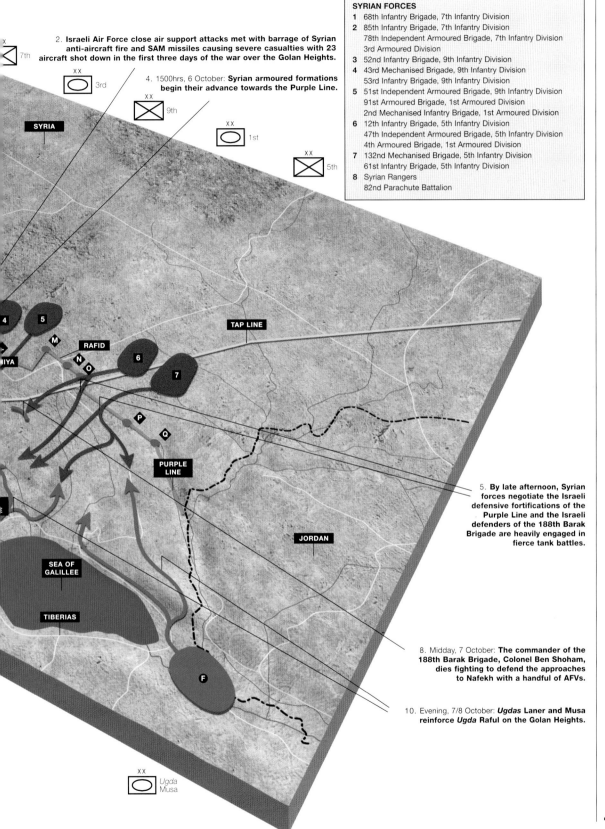

**SYRIAN FORCES**

**1** 68th Infantry Brigade, 7th Infantry Division
**2** 85th Infantry Brigade, 7th Infantry Division
   78th Independent Armoured Brigade, 7th Infantry Division
   3rd Armoured Division
**3** 52nd Infantry Brigade, 9th Infantry Division
**4** 43rd Mechanised Brigade, 9th Infantry Division
   53rd Infantry Brigade, 9th Infantry Division
**5** 51st Independent Armoured Brigade, 9th Infantry Division
   91st Armoured Brigade, 1st Armoured Division
   2nd Mechanised Infantry Brigade, 1st Armoured Division
**6** 12th Infantry Brigade, 5th Infantry Division
   47th Independent Armoured Brigade, 5th Infantry Division
   4th Armoured Brigade, 1st Armoured Division
**7** 132nd Mechanised Brigade, 5th Infantry Division
   61st Infantry Brigade, 5th Infantry Division
**8** Syrian Rangers
   82nd Parachute Battalion

2. **Israeli Air Force close air support attacks met with barrage of Syrian anti-aircraft fire and SAM missiles causing severe casualties with 23 aircraft shot down in the first three days of the war over the Golan Heights.**

4. 1500hrs, 6 October: **Syrian armoured formations begin their advance towards the Purple Line.**

SYRIA

TAP LINE

RAFID

PURPLE LINE

JORDAN

SEA OF GALILEE

TIBERIAS

5. **By late afternoon, Syrian forces negotiate the Israeli defensive fortifications of the Purple Line and the Israeli defenders of the 188th Barak Brigade are heavily engaged in fierce tank battles.**

8. Midday, 7 October: **The commander of the 188th Barak Brigade, Colonel Ben Shoham, dies fighting to defend the approaches to Nafekh with a handful of AFVs.**

10. Evening, 7/8 October: *Ugdas* Laner and Musa reinforce *Ugda* Raful on the Golan Heights.

*Ugda* Musa

wounded. Mobilisation was moving into top gear, and the Deputy Chief of General Staff, Major General Israel Tal, made a key decision to commit reserve units as soon as they were assembled. Although this ensured their speedy arrival on the Golan, it was to cause considerable command and organisational problems.

However, the situation remained critical for the IDF. Early on 7 October Moshe Dayan, the Israeli Minister of War, made flying visits to the Southern and Northern fronts. He was alarmed by the situation in the north and returned to Tel Aviv to advise the Prime Minister, Golda Meir, that the IDF must withdraw from the Golan Heights to the very edge of the escarpment overlooking the Jordan Valley.

Golda Meir turned for advice to the retired Lieutenant General Chaim Bar Lev, now Minister for Trade and Industry. Meir was well aware that a disaster in the north could have catastrophic consequences in Galilee. Bar Lev donned a uniform and, with the agreement of Generals Elazar and Dayan, hurried to Northern Command headquarters in Rosh Pina on the evening of 7 October. Elazar had authorised Bar Lev to issue emergency orders in the name of the IDF should he deem this necessary.

Noting the unmistakable air of gloom that pervaded Hofi's HQ, Bar Lev outlined the plans that had been made for the speedy mobilisation and deployment of two reserve divisions, commanded respectively by Major Generals Dan Laner and Moshe Peled, and for the interim piecemeal commitment of mobilised reserves as they arrived. Then Bar Lev drove to Laner's HQ – no more than three tanks and three APCs – at the Arik Bridge. Here he spoke briefly and persuasively to staff officers and senior commanders, instilling calm and confidence and issuing orders for a counter-attack on 8 October. In morale terms, Bar Lev's intervention was crucial.

On the evening of 7 October, Major General Laner had secured agreement to a division of responsibilities on the Golan with Eitan. The dividing line between their commands lay approximately a kilometre south of the Benot Ya'akov–Kuneitra road. Eitan was to be responsible for everything north of that line including the road, Laner for all operations to the south.

Laner had, as yet, no clear idea of what was happening on the ground for which he was now responsible, but from his forward command post, at the Arik Bridge, he could see clearly Syrian tanks barely five kilometres away. His first action had been to send the 679th Reserve Armoured Brigade, under the command of Colonel Uri Orr to support Eitan and relieve Nafekh. By nightfall, Orr had secured Nafekh after a tough encounter battle with the Syrian 91st Armoured Brigade, which was driven away to the east and south. Orr was now able to send fresh elements of his brigade north to take up position on the right flank of the 7th Armoured Brigade.

Israeli armour and infantry reinforcements pour onto the Golan Heights after the initial offensive. The World War II vintage M-3 halftrack remained the principal infantry transport vehicle in the IDF during the October War. This tank unit has a mixture of older Meteor petrol-engined Centurions and the modernised *Sho't* as it assembles near Nafekh Camp.

Laner began to reorganise his forces. The commander of the 4th Reserve Armoured Brigade was ordered to take the road south to Gamla Rise where he was joined by one of Barak's company commanders with two reserve tank companies; 19th Brigade was also ordered to move south to El Al with whatever forces were immediately available, where it was joined by another of Barak Brigade's reserve companies; 17th Brigade to the northeast, fewer than 50 tanks strong and locked in a desperate struggle on the Yehudia road, was reinforced with the tanks of a divisional reconnaissance unit bound for Eitan but commandeered by Laner. It had run into three Syrian tank brigades – 47th, 48th, 51st – and in a series of stiff actions on the Yehudia–Hushniyah road, the brigade accounted for over 50 Syrians tanks before its commander, Colonel Ran Sarig, was wounded and evacuated to the rear.

Under heavy Syrian fire, Laner himself acted as divisional traffic policeman, sending units on their way as they arrived by platoons and companies. The situation remained one of great confusion. Only prompt thinking by Laner prevented Barak units on the Gamla Rise from firing on retreating troops of the Golani Brigade under the mistaken impression they were Syrian infantry.

By 1200hrs on the 7th, Laner had committed some 60 tanks on his front, a figure that had increased to 90 by dusk. Holding the last high ground just east of the escarpment, the tanks were now engaged in a desperate struggle with the armour of the Syrian 5th Infantry Division and its attached armoured brigade. By the end of the day the southern Golan from Nafekh to the Yarmouk Valley was littered with about 250 destroyed and damaged tanks, 150 of them stopped by Laner's makeshift division.

While the outcome of the battle hung on a knife-edge in the southern Golan, the Syrian High Command was holding a fateful meeting at Katana, its field HQ 40km behind the frontline. The meeting on the afternoon of 7 October was attended by General Tlas, Major General Youssef Chakkour (Chief of Staff), General Maji Jamil (commander of the air force) and other senior officers. The meeting took a decision that had a significant influence on the October War. The Syrian forces in the southern sector of the Golan were to halt at 1700hrs, with one vital hour of daylight left. When the Syrians decided to renew their advance their chance to reach the River Jordan had gone.

Not all the Syrian formations obeyed the order but, crucially, the 1st Armoured Division did. The greater part of this unit halted, together with elements of the 5th Infantry Division, at Hushniyah. In the southernmost sector of the battlefield, on the road to El Al, two brigades of the Syrian 5th Infantry Division, 47th Armoured and 132nd Mechanised Infantry Brigades, also stopped in their tracks with the road to the Sea of Galilee wide open. Subsequently, the Israelis ascribed this decision to Syrian loss of nerve after suffering excessive casualties, fuel shortages and a breakdown in morale. There is no evidence of a loss of morale, although it is clear that the IAF had managed to interdict Syrian fuel and ammunition supplies. A partial explanation, however, was the perceived need to reorganise after heavy fighting. This would certainly apply to 1st Armoured Division, whose every move to break through at Nafekh had been blocked by Eitan. However, another explanation particularly relevant to the failure to exploit at El Al is that the Syrians were, as has already been noted, 'playing by the

Virtually every Israeli tank was mobilised during the October War including the venerable Sherman, which the Israelis had modified with French smoothbore 75mm and 105mm guns. Both proved capable of destroying the T-54/55 tanks that equipped the majority of the Syrian armoured formations.

book'. Thus, having reached a particular line, they waited for follow-up units to move through them despite the lack of Israeli opposition. Having run into such dogged resistance to the north in the Valley of Tears, both the southern commanders and the Syrian High Command were concerned about a devastating flank attack on 5th Infantry and 1st Armoured Divisions.

Tlas was to compound this error by committing his reserve 3rd Armoured Division to the attack in the north, where the Israeli defence was holding, rather than reinforce success in the south. In fact, Tlas achieved the worst of all possible results by splitting the 3rd Armoured Division both to reinforce the 7th Infantry Division in the fight for Booster and to support the 9th Infantry Division in a bid to outflank Rafid and link up with the 1st Armoured Division. He had committed the cardinal sin of failing to maintain the operation's aim and was to pay dearly for it.

On the evening of 7 October, the leading units of Major General Moshe Peled's 146th Reserve Armoured Division were moving up the El Al road. Initially, there had been some disagreement within the Israeli high command over the deployment of Peled's division. It had been proposed that the division should concentrate at the Benot Ya'akov Bridge. Peled had opposed this first option, on the grounds that he had few transporters. His division had already been travelling a long time on tracks and to reach the Benot Ya'akov would require yet more punishing track mileage. Peled urged that he be allowed to attack along the El Al axis, and the southern route was confirmed by Hofi with the backing of Bar Lev. Barely 36 hours after the opening of the Syrian offensive, the IDF was about to launch a major counter-attack.

## THE VALLEY OF TEARS

At 0800hrs on 7 October, the Syrians went on the attack again in the Valley of Tears. The 78th Armoured Brigade of the 7th Infantry Division advanced along a three-kilometre front between Booster and Mount Hermonit, aiming to push a force up the wadi running along the base of Hermonit towards Wasset. Colonel Avigdor Ben Gal conducted a masterful defence, conserving his forces and always retaining a reserve. He stayed in

Colonel Avigdor Ben Gal, known to his troops as 'Yanush', was the commander of the 7th Armoured Brigade during the fighting on the Golan Heights. His intuitive and inspired decision to order his company commanders to reconnoitre the area prior to the war was arguably the difference between victory and defeat. Equally inspired was his conduct during the battle. Throughout he managed to retain a tactical reserve, however small, to counter repeated Syrian breakthroughs. He paid a high personal price; the immense stress of the fighting on the Northern Front led to a heart attack after the war. Fortunately, he survived this individual battle and recovered to reach the rank of Major General and subsequently became the chairman of Israeli Defense Industries.

constant touch with Eitan as the battle progressed. The 7th Brigade was soon fighting at ranges that varied from point-blank to 2,500m. The attack lasted some four hours and then the Syrians withdrew, leaving more mangled armour on the valley floor. Plumes of smoke hung over knocked-out tanks.

While the 71st Battalion remained in the northern sector, the 77th OZ Battalion was moved from south of Kuneitra to a central position overlooking the Valley of Tears at Hermonit. The battalion commander, Lieutenant Colonel Avigdor Kahalani, left a company behind in the Kuneitra sector, guarding the brigade's flank, and during the afternoon it came under heavy Syrian attack. Once again the Syrians were driven off, leaving 20 tanks behind them.

At 2200hrs, the Syrians launched a night attack in Ben Gal's central sector preceded by a massive artillery bombardment. The Syrian 7th Infantry Division had now been augmented by the 3rd Armoured Division, whose 81st Armoured Brigade was equipped with T-62 tanks. Kahalani had at his disposal some 40 tanks to pit against the Syrians' 500. Using its night-fighting equipment, the Syrian armour closed to ranges of 50m while infantry equipped with RPGs attempted to infiltrate the Israeli lines. The fighting reached a climax at about 0100hrs on the 8th and then abruptly ceased as the Syrians scurried about the battlefield, attempting to evacuate their wounded and their damaged tanks. The Israelis laid down heavy artillery fire as their own tanks were refuelled and reloaded.

The Syrians attacked again at 0400hrs and, as the sky grew lighter, an increasingly nightmarish scene was revealed in the Valley of Tears. Many of the abandoned or wrecked Syrian tanks and APCs were between or behind the Israeli positions. The extent of 7th Armoured Brigade's plight was all too evident and Ben Gal ordered the brigade to fire at every moving target in sight.

The Syrians were suffering too. Brigadier General Omar Abrash, commanding the 7th Infantry Division, withdrew the battered units of his first echelon and committed the second echelon, planning to take advantage of the Syrian night-vision equipment. At dusk, while readying his armour for attack, Abrash was killed when his command tank took a direct hit. This setback undoubtedly dealt a severe blow to Syrian morale and the attack was postponed to the morning of 9 October. At about 0900hrs, after an accurate artillery barrage, the Syrians attempted to force their way through the Valley of Tears towards the high ground between Mount Hermonit and Booster.

The preliminary Syrian bombardment had been so intense that Ben Gal had ordered the tanks of the 77th Battalion to leave the ridge where they occupied a natural firing ramp and fall back 500m, anticipating that there would be sufficient time for them to regain their positions once the bombardment had lifted. But the Syrians moved too fast, seizing the crest where the 77th Armoured Battalion had been positioned and threatening a breakthrough. The outcome of the battle now hung in the balance. Suddenly a force of Syrian Mi-8 helicopters swooped over the armoured slogging match on the ridgeline, heading west to land a raiding party of commandos near El Rom. Shortly afterwards, Eitan received a report that a body of Syrian infantry was advancing to the north of El Rom. The drive on El Rom had also been joined by the T-62s of Assad's Republican Guard, which had pushed up the wadi below

Hermonit and past the Israeli frontline. If the Syrian armour could link up with the infantry in the El Rom sector, there was nothing to stand between them and Kiryat Shmona in northern Israel.

Ben Gal attempted to block the Republican Guards with the tanks of his 71st Battalion, which was holding the northern sector of the battlefield. Within minutes of engaging the Syrians, however, the battalion commander, Lieutenant Colonel Ratess, was killed. Ben Gal then ordered Lieutenant Colonel Kahalani, commanding 77th Battalion, to assume command of the remnants of 71st Battalion. Manoeuvring his 15 tanks on high ground overlooking the valley and firing from ramps, Kahalani's force halted the Republican Guard at ranges that never exceeded 500m. Some of the Syrian tanks managed to throw off the stranglehold and move behind the Israelis as the battle dissolved into a swirling melee of individual duels fought in a cauldron of smoke and flames laced with the reek of burning cordite. The Israeli tank crews had been in action for four days and three nights and, on average, were now down to their last four shells.

Ben Gal radioed Eitan that he did not think that 7th Brigade could hold on any longer. He had started the battle with 105 tanks and now had just seven left. Eitan tried to calm him, promising that he would soon be receiving reinforcements. The Syrians, sensing victory, were pushing past the line of abandoned Israeli ramps, but there now occurred another of those remarkable incidents on which the fate of armies turns.

When the war broke out, Lieutenant Colonel Yosi Ben Hannan, a former commander of the 53rd Battalion within the Barak Brigade, had been on his honeymoon in the Himalayas. On being told of the outbreak of war, Ben Hannan had used enormous initiative to fly back to Israel via Teheran and Athens, telephoning his family from the Greek capital to bring his uniform to Lod airport. From Lod, Ben Hannan had

**A Centurion lies burnt out and gutted after a massive internal explosion rent the tank asunder. This unmodified petrol-engined version of the Centurion was more susceptible to fire than the *Sho't* Upgraded Centurion with its diesel engine. Statistically, every Israeli tank deployed on the Golan Heights was hit one and a half times and 250 were knocked out, although all but 100 were subsequently returned to operational status.**

**STAFF SERGEANT AMIR BASHARI, 2ND PLATOON, 3RD COMPANY, 77TH BATTALION, 7TH ARMOURED BRIGADE, OVERLOOKING THE VALLEY OF TEARS, EVENING, SATURDAY 6 OCTOBER 1973** (pages 56–57)

The majority of the personnel of the 7th Armoured Brigade were young conscripts of 19 or 20 years of age who had never been in combat before. Although an elite formation within the Israeli Armoured Corps, the 7th Armoured Brigade had trained extensively for war in the Sinai Desert and was deployed to the Golan Heights just days before the outbreak of the October War. Staff Sergeant Amir Bashari was a veteran platoon sergeant in the 7th Armoured Brigade with only a matter of weeks left before his service was complete. As the commander of *Sho't* 'Beta 1' (1) within 3rd or H Company of the 77th OZ Battalion, Bashari had commented to his company commander, Lt Avraham 'Emmy' Palant, and his battalion commander, LtCol Avigdor Kahalani, on the morning of 6 October that he was fed up with firing at barrels during gunnery practice. His years of experience were soon to be tested to the full. As the 7th Armoured Brigade deployed to the frontlines, H Company was transferred to the 75th Mechanised Infantry Battalion under the command of LtCol Yos Eldar at the Waset Junction. Bashari and his platoon took up station near the commanding feature of Tel Hermonit. It lay right in the path of the advancing Syrian 7th Infantry Division (2). H Company found itself fighting the Syrians at odds of over 15:1. Battle was joined with the Israeli tanks on their firing ramps subjected to devastating artillery fire. Bashari's gunner, Moshe Uliel, exacted a fearful toll of Syrian tanks

but the odds were overwhelming. Despite coming under fire from the guns of numerous tanks and artillery pieces, Bashari did not retreat. At 2130hrs, an artillery shell exploded on the exterior of his tank and Bashari was killed instantly, his body slumping inside the turret. Bashari was the first fatality within the 7th Armoured Brigade. Almost 60 per cent of the casualties within armoured brigades on the Golan Heights were tank commanders. It is standard procedure for Israeli tank commanders to operate with their head out of the turret for better observation. However, so many were decapitated by shell fire in the first day of the war that tank crews were ordered to wear their dogtags around their ankles so that headless bodies could be identified. The sight of their tank commander's headless torso collapsing into the fighting compartment was too much for most crews and many, understandably, abandoned their tank. Bashari's gunner and loader, Uliel and Ganani, jumped out of 'Beta 1' and took shelter among the rocks. When recovered, such tanks were virtually undamaged but the congealed blood splashed around the inside of the turret made it impossible for replacement crews to man the tank. The Israeli repair teams quickly found cleaning using diesel fuel overpowered the smell. This allowed the tanks to be returned to service as quickly as possible. Bashari was posthumously awarded the Medal of Gallantry. Bashari's *Sho't* is shown here with the insignia of the 7th Armoured Brigade (3) on the rear hull although this was not normally carried in combat for security reasons. The registration number on this tank (4) is not that of 'Beta 1' but of the Centurion memorial on the Golan Heights. (Howard Gerrard)

gone straight to the workshops behind the Golan front. Here teams were working round the clock on battle-damaged tanks. Ben Hannan collected 13 battleworthy vehicles and assembled sufficient crews to man them, including some wounded volunteers who had discharged themselves from hospital. With his small band of battered tanks, he headed for the 7th Armoured Brigade's sector.

Eitan had hastily placed Ben Hannan under the command of Ben Gal, who was on the point of ordering a withdrawal when his small task force arrived. Ben Gal's seven remaining tanks, now virtually out of ammunition, joined Ben Hannan's force as the latter went on to the counter-attack, breasting the rise southeast of Booster to slam into the Syrian left flank. In the first clash Ben Hannan's force destroyed some 30 Syrian tanks. A report came in from A3, one of the Israeli strongpoints isolated but intact on the Purple Line, that the Syrian supply columns were pulling back. The Syrians, who had fought themselves to a standstill between Hermonit and Booster, began to withdraw under a huge pall of dust while the Israelis tracked them in cautious pursuit. The arrival of Ben Hannan's tanks on the battlefield must have seemed to the battle-weary Syrians a preliminary to the arrival of yet more fresh Israeli reserve formations. Later Ben Gal observed: 'You never know the condition of the other side. You always assume he is in better shape than you. The Syrians, apparently, assumed that they had no chance of success. They did not know the truth, that our situation was desperate.'

The battle for the Booster feature was over. Eitan spoke over the radio to Ben Gal and his men, saying, 'You have saved the people of Israel.' The survivors of the 7th Armoured Brigade had been without sleep for 80 hours and had fought continuously for over 50 hours. They had lost all but seven of their tanks. In the Valley of Tears, however, they had knocked out 260 Syrian tanks and 500 other vehicles. The ground over which they fought – some 15km wide and 3km deep – had been rigorously prepared for battle and the range tables, ramps and alternative positions had been sited and constructed to enable a heavily outnumbered force to fight a holding action. Moreover, Ben Gal's handling of his mobile reserves was

assured in retaining control of the high ground and the killing grounds in the valley below it.

Not even Ben Gal, however, could have anticipated the ferocity of the fighting, the odds at which it would be fought and the physical and moral demands this would make. The defensive nature of the battle exposed the IDF to the full fury of Syrian artillery, which took a punitive toll of the tank commanders of the 7th Armoured Brigade, while the Syrian armour's night-vision equipment gave it a huge tactical advantage that crucially it failed to exploit fully. The savagery of the battle also underlined the vulnerability of Israeli commanders as they directed the battle from open tank hatches under heavy fire.

The narrow margin of victory in the Valley of Tears was also a brutal reminder of the failure of the IDF to mobilise its reserves in time to meet the magnitude of the threat to Israel on the Golan. In the opening phase of the battle, the Barak and 7th Armoured Brigades were the only armoured elements of the IDF with which the Syrians had to contend. Had they been faced with all the brigades eventually dispatched to the Northern Front, the outcome would have been clear cut. There would have been a repetition of the Valley of Tears along the Purple Line.

### The Israeli Air Force

The Israeli Air Force entered the war with every confidence that it could provide the essential close air support for the ground forces. It was to suffer a fearful shock as the first Skyhawk was downed by a SAM-6 missile within minutes. The comprehensive Arab air defence system caused heavy Israeli losses on both the Northern and Southern fronts – some 50 aircraft – in the first two days, amounting to almost 15 per cent of its frontline strength. The IAF kept flying by employing a wide variety of tactics including contour flying and evasive manoeuvring, the Sam Song warning system,

A mortally wounded Israeli tank commander is gently lowered from the turret of his *Sho't* tank after he was struck in the throat by fragments from an exploding Sagger missile. Almost two-thirds of the Israeli Armoured Corps fatalities on the Golan Heights were tank commanders. Necessarily the brightest and the best within both the army and society, their loss was felt all the more keenly by the state of Israel. Israeli losses on the Golan Heights during the October War were 772 dead and 2,453 wounded in just 18 days of fighting.

An Israeli F-4 Phantom plunges earthwards after being hit by Syrian anti-aircraft fire. On 7 October, six Israeli Phantoms were shot out of the sky by Syrian air defences and 33 Phantoms were lost during the course of the war. The Israelis lost 51 aircraft over the Golan Heights with 23 of the 51 downed in the first three days of the war. Total losses in the war amounted to 103 Israeli aircraft, of which just five were shot down in air-to-air combat as against Israeli claims of 277 Arab planes destroyed in dogfights.

**Bombs rain down on the airbase of Nazaria as the Israeli Air Force strikes deep into Syria seeking to emasculate its opponent. The Syrian Air Force mustered some 250 operational combat jets on six main airbases; all were subjected to concerted attacks by the *Heyl Ha'avir* or Israeli Air Force.**

flares, chaff and electronic countermeasures [ECM] to overcome the threat posed to low-flying aircraft by the SAM-6s and ZSU-23-4 self-propelled anti-aircraft guns.

Before the war, the IAF had not known the frequencies used by the SAM-6. It took some time to discover them and make appropriate adjustments to the ECM pods used by its aircraft, which succeeded in neutralising the active radar mode but not the optical sight. The IAF's problems were compounded by the loss of the Mount Hermon observation post and radar station on the opening day of the War.

The losses sustained in the first two days of fighting forced the IAF to reduce the tempo of close air support and attempt to neutralise the SAM sites. It was a costly and brutal battle. In one operation alone the IAF lost six aircraft while destroying only one Syrian SAM site. On 8 October, the IAF began bombing Syrian airbases; within a week most of them were inoperable. On 9 October, in response to the Syrian firing of some 10 FROG missiles at targets in Israel including the Ramat David airbase, the IAF launched a strategic offensive against Syria. First they destroyed the Barouk radar station in Lebanon, which was linked to the Syrian network, in order to open new attack routes and as a warning to other Arab neighbours of Israel. The IAF then launched a comprehensive attack on the Syrian oil industry and electric power generating system. Also targeted were the oil port of Banias, the refineries at Homs and oil storage depots throughout Syria.

Israel later claimed to have attacked only strategic targets, but on 9 October a successful raid flown by eight F-4 Phantoms against the Syrian Air Force headquarters in Damascus also hit buildings nearby in the city's diplomatic quarter, causing a number of casualties. One of the Phantoms was lost during this mission and a second wave of F-4s was diverted, because of cloud cover over Damascus, to bomb Syrian troop concentrations near Hushniyah.

On the morning of 9 October, when bad news was still coming in from the Northern and Southern fronts, the Israeli War Cabinet discussed a more drastic form of air attack – the possible use of nuclear weapons. Some accounts of this meeting allege that Dayan and Meir ordered the arming of Israel's missiles with nuclear warheads and that nuclear weapons were loaded onto a squadron of F-4s at Tel Nof airbase in the heart of Israel. This may have been a stratagem to speed up the American resupply of the IDF. This operation got under way on the night of 13 October with the launching of a massive airlift.

Once it had recovered its balance one of the aims of the IAF was, as David Elazar put it, to force the Syrians to 'scream stop' by destroying the strategic infrastructure on which their war-making capacity depended. To reduce Israel's vulnerability it was axiomatic that their Arab enemies had to be dealt severe blows, the economic consequences of which would be felt for years.

בפגיעה

## Israel Stabilises the Golan Front

On the evening of Sunday 7 October, Colonel Tewfiq Juhni, the commander of the Syrian 1st Armoured Division, established a supply and administrative complex in the area of Hushniyah. Juhni was confident that an advance into Israel would be made on the following day. The Israelis had other ideas. When the sun came up on Monday the IDF was ready to seize the initiative. Major General Yitzhak Hofi, GOC Northern Command, planned to isolate the Syrian penetration with converging blows delivered by *Ugdas* Laner and Musa. It was the Israeli advance along the road towards El Al that alerted Colonel Juhni to the danger that now threatened his division.

At 2000hrs on Sunday 7 October, Peled had briefed an orders group at Tzemach at the southern end of the Sea of Galilee. He planned to attack on two routes: the main effort was to be put in by the 9th Reserve Armoured Brigade along the El Al–Rafid road. The 205th Reserve Armoured Brigade would follow up this attack, while the 70th Reserve Armoured Brigade mopped up and shielded the right flank of the advance above the Ruqqad escarpment. On the left flank of the main effort, the 4th Reserve Armoured Brigade was tasked with advancing from the Gamla Rise at Givat Yoav through Mazrat Kuneitra to Hushniyah. Peled's counter-attack went in at 0830hrs on Monday 8 October. By noon, *Ugda* Musa had reached Tel Faris after heavy fighting, with some 50 Syrian tanks destroyed between Ramat Magshimim and El Al, a distance of some nine kilometres.

The 205th Reserve Armoured Brigade then struck north, while the 9th Reserve Armoured Brigade refuelled and protected the left flank of the advance. Peled then ordered 19th Reserve Armoured Brigade to push up the lateral road that ran north from Magshimim to move on to the left

flank of 4th Reserve Armoured Brigade and broaden the divisional front. By 1300hrs, Peled's armour had reached the point at Juhader intersected by the TAP line road. By this time the lead battalion of the 205th Reserve Armoured Brigade had advanced to Tel Saki on the road to Juhader. Here they ran into strong Syrian anti-tank defence consisting of hedgehogs of Saggers, tanks and anti-tank guns located on both sides of the road and covered by heavy concentrations of artillery fire. The lead battalion was pinned down by the weight of Syrian fire and the 205th Reserve Armoured Brigade was forced to launch a major attack to retrieve the situation.

The strength and depth of the Syrian defences surprised Peled and his brigade commanders. In the late afternoon, however, 9th Reserve Armoured Brigade, moving up on the 4th Reserve Armoured Brigade's left, burst through an anti-tank position that the Syrians had not yet completed. By the evening of 8 October the Syrians had withdrawn from Juhader, exposing the Syrian 1st Armoured Division's supply lines running south along the TAP line and forcing Juhni to commit an armoured brigade the next morning to secure the route.

Meanwhile, throughout 8 October, Major General Laner's division was fighting its way eastward against mounting opposition. The depleted 17th Reserve Armoured Brigade was slogging up the Yehudia road towards the TAP line through a succession of Syrian ambushes and had been reduced to one tank battalion and an attached reconnaissance unit destined for *Ugda* Raful. To the north, the 679th Reserve Armoured Brigade was locked in battle with Syrian forces pressing up the TAP line to overrun Nafekh.

Laner was exerting pressure on Juhni's 1st Armoured Division, which was still moving northward along the TAP line road and westward towards the Jordan. Juhni was an able and hard-driving commander and, in contrast to the generally cautious performance of the Syrian Army, had subordinates who were not afraid to use their initiative. Colonel Shafiq Fayad, commander of the 91st Armoured Brigade, was one such. He had bypassed the stubbornly defended base at Nafekh to strike west across country and push his forward elements to within reach of Snobar, the main IDF supply depot on the Golan escarpment. Some of Juhni's forward elements almost reached the old Customs House only five kilometres from the River Jordan. This was the deepest Syrian penetration of the war and just a ten-minute tank drive from the Benot Ya'akov Bridge

The fighting for the TAP line was intense. Moving south down the TAP line road, the 679th Reserve Armoured Brigade, reinforced by a company detached from the 7th Brigade to the north, drove the Syrians from Sindiana and by nightfall controlled the TAP line road around Nafekh. There was more hard fighting for the 679th Reserve Armoured Brigade on the morning of 9 October when the Syrians counter-attacked after a heavy artillery bombardment. The Syrian assault was broken up at long range by Israeli tank fire. That afternoon, as the 17th Reserve Armoured Brigade closed on the TAP line from the west, the 679th Reserve Armoured Brigade moved on Hushniyah, the headquarters of the 1st Armoured Division and defended in depth by tanks, anti-tank guns, missiles and infantry armed with RPGs.

**Israeli armour advances alongside the chain-link fencing of the TAP line road. This was one of the main Syrian axes of advance in the opening battles of the war. The attack was only thwarted by the tenacity and courage of a handful of Israeli tank crews during the first desperate night of the war.**

As night closed in on 8 October, Colonel Uri Orr took Tel Ramtania, a heavily fortified spur of the Hushniyah defensive box. Orr's brigade had taken heavy losses in a day of continuous fighting that had seen the birth of a new esprit de corps. By the evening of Tuesday 9 October, Laner had shut the northern and western pincers on the Syrian concentration at Hushniyah. The 679th Reserve Armoured Brigade looked down on it from Tel Ramtania and the 17th Reserve Armoured Brigade was on the TAP line road, refuelling and poised to move east. Peled was to close the trap from the southeast.

In the small hours of 9 October, Peled briefed his orders group on their line of advance. The 205th Reserve Armoured Brigade was to advance on the Syrian border, keeping the Rafid–Tel Faris road on its left; the 14th Reserve Armoured Brigade was to press on to the left of the El Al–Rafid road; and 19th Brigade was to drive on Hushniyah. Peled intended that his division's impetus would carry him across the ceasefire line, taking Tel Kudne in the process. It was the first time since his division had joined the battle that Peled was able to brief all his subordinate commanders, an indication that order was being restored to the battlefield.

When the attack went in at dawn, Peled collided with the Syrian 46th Armoured Brigade covering the southern flank of the 1st Armoured Division, now fighting for its life around Hushniyah. On his right flank, amid emotional scenes, Peled had linked up with the garrisons of those IDF strongpoints that had held out since the beginning of the war. Meanwhile the 9th Reserve Armoured Brigade was swinging northwest to close on Hushniyah. Linking with *Ugda* Laner advancing from the west, the Israelis reached the high ground southeast of Hushniyah by mid-morning on 9 October. Heavy fighting ensued with a Syrian force of some 50 tanks augmented with anti-tank guns and missiles. The Israelis suffered heavy losses and the attack was brought to a halt.

To the south, better progress was being made against the 46th Syrian Armoured Brigade by the 205th Reserve Armoured Brigade, which by 1200hrs had reached the area of Tel Faris. However, the 205th Reserve Armoured Brigade was in a dangerously exposed position. Syrian armour was being fed across the Purple Line, and Peled's division was now straddled alarmingly across its three principal axes of advance.

The Syrians, however, were also facing tough choices. The 91st Armoured Brigade had been pummelled by the 679th Reserve Brigade and was no longer an effective fighting formation. North of Kuneitra, the Syrians were unable to break through. Before developing this phase of operations, Juhni, commander of the Syrian 1st Armoured Division, had established his divisional supply system around Hushniyah as a preliminary to breaking in to Israel itself. However, he was now threatened by Laner's forces from the west and north and Peled's forces from the south. The tables had been turned on Juhni, and his division was threatened with envelopment.

The Syrian plight was compounded by the increasing effectiveness of the IAF, which had largely overcome the Syrian SAM threat and brought the Hushniyah pocket under effective bombardment. Juhni ordered his forces to attack Peled's arm of the pincer to break the stranglehold. Peled, meanwhile, ordered the 4th Reserve Armoured Brigade to make an all-out attack in the centre in which it seized control of the Hushniyah–Rafid road, easing the pressure on the left flank of 205th Reserve Armoured Brigade, which overran Tel Faris and gained an excellent observation post. The tactical advantage this conferred was, however, mitigated by the fact that a small number of Syrian troops managed to remain in hiding on Tel Faris and were able to direct Syrian fire until 11 October, when they were eliminated. Peled's attack was, nevertheless, developing according to plan, and he now ordered the 9th Reserve Armoured Brigade to move on Hushniyah with close air and artillery support. The attack broke through the Syrian positions, taking the high ground at Tel Fazra, but again encountering stubborn Syrian resistance. After darkness fell, the Syrians began to infiltrate back, and the fighting became confused. The Syrian 15th Mechanised Infantry Brigade, detached from the 3rd Armoured Division and moved to reinforce the main effort in the south, tried to punch its way through to the 1st Armoured Division in the Hushniyah pocket but was blocked at Tel Faris by the 205th Reserve Armoured Brigade.

Peled held an orders group in the small hours of Wednesday 10 October and reaffirmed the overall aim of seizing Tel Kudne, the Syrian forward HQ some 15km to the northeast of Tel Faris, which was now held by the 205th Reserve Armoured Brigade along with the Rafid crossroads. Although Peled was still baulked in the area of Hushniyah, where the 9th Reserve Armoured Brigade was heavily engaged, he was moving steadily up to the ceasefire line.

Peled's thrust on Tel Kudne ran into determined Syrian opposition. He was ordered by Hofi to remain on the defensive, to provide the anvil against which the Syrian pocket could be crushed by the hammer of Laner's division attacking from the north with 679th and 17th Reserve Armoured Brigades. When Laner and Peled's forward units met near Hushniyah, the entire area became a vast tank-killing ground. Two brigades of the Syrian 1st Armoured Division had been destroyed, turning the Hushniyah pocket into a colossal mechanical graveyard of burnt-out tanks, artillery, APCs, trucks and stores. The remnants of the Syrian Army streamed east over the ceasefire line, and by nightfall there was not a single Syrian unit on territory west of the Purple Line.

On the Golan plateau, the Syrians had left behind some 870 tanks, many of them T-62s, hundreds of guns and APCs, thousands of vehicles and enormous quantities of equipment. The carefully prepared Soviet-style offensive, launched on 6 October, had ended in crushing defeat and the Syrians were back on their start line.

# THE ISRAELI COUNTER-ATTACK

On the night of 10 October, the Israeli Cabinet, advised by its Chief of Staff General Elazar, had to decide whether to exploit its success against Syria or to concentrate against Egypt. The General Staff was also considering its options. There were several trenchant arguments in favour of adopting the first course of action. First, if the Syrian Army could be broken, it would then be safe to concentrate against Egypt, mainspring of the Arab alliance. Second, on 10 October Iraq had sent two armoured divisions to help the Syrians and had moved approximately 100 warplanes to advanced bases in western Iraq. There was also still a possibility that Jordan might intervene. On 10 October, Jordan had announced that it was calling up reservists and mobilising its resources for the 'war effort'. The IDF defences along the

The Israelis have never been able to afford many special-purpose AFV variants. However, several M48 AVLB bridgelayers were employed during the Israeli counteroffensive, both to cross the Israeli anti-tank ditch at the Purple Line and to overcome Syrian obstacles on the approaches to Damascus.

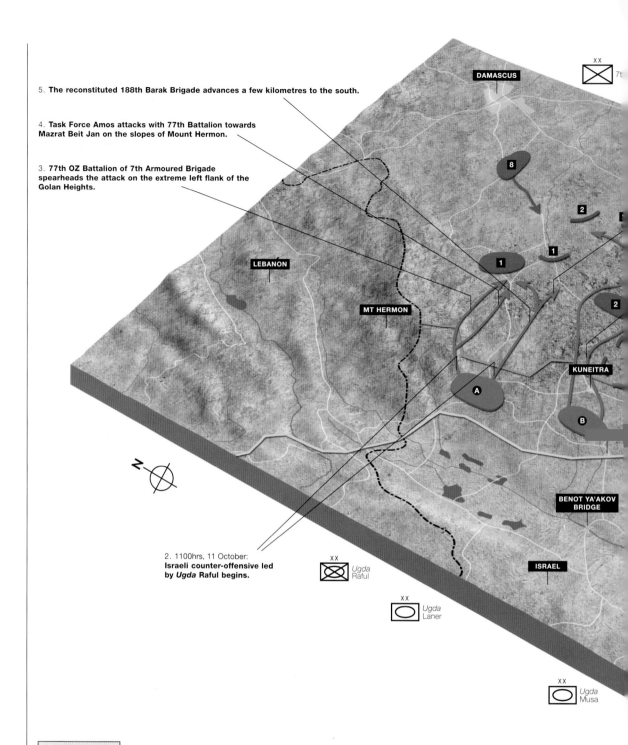

5. **The reconstituted 188th Barak Brigade advances a few kilometres to the south.**

4. **Task Force Amos attacks with 77th Battalion towards Mazrat Beit Jan on the slopes of Mount Hermon.**

3. **77th OZ Battalion of 7th Armoured Brigade spearheads the attack on the extreme left flank of the Golan Heights.**

DAMASCUS

7t

8

2

1

1

2

LEBANON

MT HERMON

2

KUNEITRA

A

B

BENOT YA'AKOV BRIDGE

N

ISRAEL

2. 1100hrs, 11 October: **Israeli counter-offensive led by Ugda Raful begins.**

XX *Ugda* Raful

XX *Ugda* Laner

XX *Ugda* Musa

**ISRAELI FORCES**
| | |
|---|---|
| A | *Ugda* Raful |
| B | *Ugda* Laner |
| C | *Ugda* Musa |

# THE ISRAELI COUNTEROFFENSIVE INTO SYRIA

11–13 October 1973, viewed from the south-west, showing the Israeli counteroffensive on the northern Golan Heights along the Damascus road.

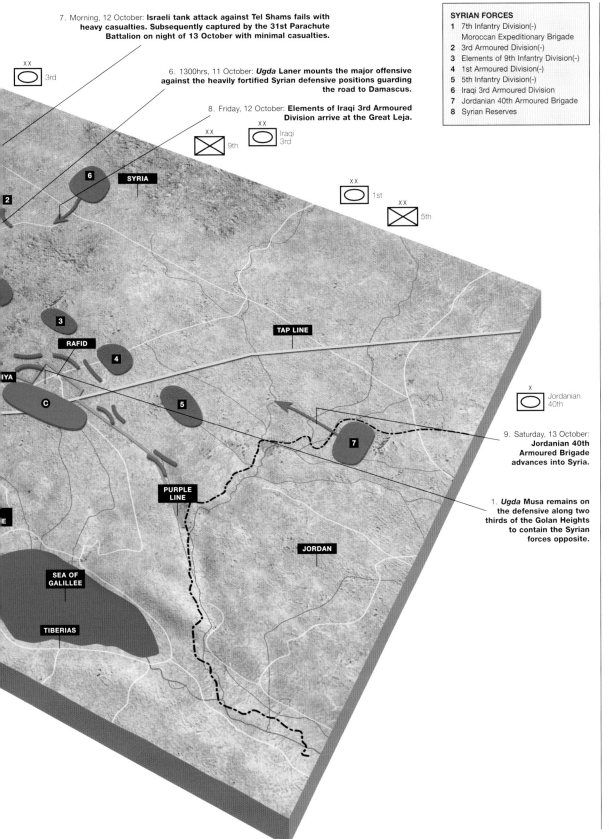

7. Morning, 12 October: **Israeli tank attack against Tel Shams fails with heavy casualties. Subsequently captured by the 31st Parachute Battalion on night of 13 October with minimal casualties.**

6. 1300hrs, 11 October: *Ugda* Laner mounts the major offensive against the heavily fortified Syrian defensive positions guarding the road to Damascus.

8. Friday, 12 October: **Elements of Iraqi 3rd Armoured Division arrive at the Great Leja.**

XX 3rd

XX 9th

XX Iraqi 3rd

XX 1st

XX 5th

6

SYRIA

2

3

RAFID

4

TAP LINE

IYA

C

5

X Jordanian 40th

7

9. Saturday, 13 October: **Jordanian 40th Armoured Brigade advances into Syria.**

PURPLE LINE

JORDAN

1. *Ugda* Musa remains on the defensive along two thirds of the Golan Heights to contain the Syrian forces opposite.

SEA OF GALILLEE

E

TIBERIAS

**SYRIAN FORCES**
1  7th Infantry Division(-)
   Moroccan Expeditionary Brigade
2  3rd Armoured Division(-)
3  Elements of 9th Infantry Division(-)
4  1st Armoured Division(-)
5  5th Infantry Division(-)
6  Iraqi 3rd Armoured Division
7  Jordanian 40th Armoured Brigade
8  Syrian Reserves

**69**

The October War was the first major clash in the history of naval warfare when both sides were armed with ship-to-ship missiles. At the outbreak of war the Israeli Navy was at battle stations and quickly gained the initiative against the Syrians. At the battle of Latakia, one Reshef and four Saar class missile boats, using sophisticated electronic countermeasures, foiled the Soviet Styx anti-ship missiles of the Syrian Osa-Class boats while the Israeli Gabriel missiles destroyed five Syrian vessels and forced the rest of the Syrian navy back into port for the remainder of the war. This despite the fact that the Styx missile had twice the range of the Gabriel.

River Jordan had been stripped and were now manned by a skeleton force. Finally, the Soviet Union was re-supplying the Syrians, who should be deterred from launching another offensive.

There were two reasons for not advancing into Syria. First, any Israeli threat to Damascus might provoke Soviet intervention. Second, the IDF ran the risk of being drawn into a battle of attrition in the deeply echeloned Syrian defensive system and the broken lava country that blocked the main axis of advance to Damascus.

The General Staff's recommendations, which were conveyed by Moshe Dayan to Golda Meir, were to advance across the ceasefire line to achieve a penetration 20km in depth and form a defensive enclave, bringing Damascus within the reach of long-range artillery. It was hoped in this way to inflict a crushing defeat on the Syrians while not provoking Soviet intervention. Golda Meir gave her assent. Confirmatory orders were then sent to Hofi and detailed planning began immediately.

It was Hofi's intention to give the Syrians no time to recover. In turn this meant attacking with forces that had little or no time either to reorganise after hard and exhausting fighting or to absorb reinforcements of men and equipment. In Eitan's 36th Armoured Division, Ben Gal's 7th Armoured Brigade had been reconstituted and reinforced with fresh troops from reserve battalions and had also absorbed the remnants of the 188th Barak Brigade, which had fought itself to a standstill and was now commanded by the redoubtable Lieutenant Colonel Ben Hannan.

Hofi planned to attack in echelon from the northernmost sector in the Golan. The left flank of the attacking forces would rest on the slopes of Mount Hermon that were impassable to armour. The axis of advance was on the shortest route to Damascus and it was anticipated that this would influence the Syrian deployment. The Israelis also correctly anticipated that the northern sector was less heavily defended by the Syrians. Eitan's reconstituted division was to lead off on the axis Majdal

Shams–Mazrat Beit Jan in the foothills of Mount Hermon. From this wooded high ground, Eitan could direct artillery and tank fire to the south in support of Laner's armoured division as it pushed forward, abreast of Eitan, along the main Kuneitra–Damascus highway two hours later.

H-Hour was fixed for 1100hrs 11 October, to allow time for reorganisation and the issuing of orders and also to avoid the tank gunners being blinded by the sun. South of Kuneitra, Peled's armoured division was to consolidate along two-thirds of the frontline and to reinforce Laner with the 9th Reserve Armoured Brigade. The Israeli plan was based on economy of effort in the centre and south in order to achieve a concentration of force in the north so as to menace Damascus and force the Syrians to give battle. Eitan's division on the left would make the main effort, but once a breakthrough had been achieved, Laner would exploit, either by passing through Eitan or by pushing for a separate breakthrough along the road to Damascus.

On the other side of the hill, the Syrian High Command was now exhibiting signs of mounting alarm. The badly mauled Syrian Army was now facing a reinvigorated enemy about to strike into its territory. The IAF was now unlocking the secret of the Syrian SAMs and inflicting heavy tactical and strategic damage on the Syrian infrastructure that in turn was hindering a concerted drive by the Soviets to re-supply their allies. The bulk of the Syrian Army was now concentrated on the approaches to Damascus while Arab allies – Moroccan, Saudi, Iraqi and Jordanian – were being assigned the role of delaying the Israeli drive.

Assad appealed to Sadat for help. But this plea was undermined by the fact that a few days earlier, when Syrian forces were poised on the

**Belching clouds of diesel exhaust, *Sho'ts* manoeuvre into formation as the Israelis mount a counter-attack against Syrian positions. The major Israeli counteroffensive into Syria began on 11 October, just five days after the start of the war. In the vanguard of the attack were the combined remnants of the 7th and 188th Barak Brigades that had borne the brunt of the Syrian offensive.**

western edge of the Golan escarpment, Assad had attempted to secure a ceasefire through the offices of the Soviet Union. His aim had been to forestall precisely the kind of Israeli counter-attack with which he was now threatened and retain control of the Golan Heights. At first Sadat, having achieved his strategic aim of a lodgement on the eastern bank of the Suez Canal, was unwilling to move, but the mounting pressure on Syria forced him to act. The armoured offensive in the Sinai, launched on 14 October, was the Egyptian response to the Syrian plight. However, it was to prove the undoing of the Egyptians. Venturing beyond its SAM umbrella, the Egyptian armour was shot to pieces and the initiative in the Sinai passed to the Israelis.

On the night of 10 October, after the command orders group, Ben Gal assembled his commanders. The events of the last four days lent his words an added layer of meaning. He told his officers that the break-in to Syria would enable them to avenge the death of their comrades who had fallen in the desperate defence of Israel. For the attack on the following day, Ben Gal deployed four tank battalions, which he allocated evenly to the Mazrat Beit Jan and Tel Shams objectives. Under cover of artillery and air strikes, the 7th Armoured Brigade broke through the Syrian minefields and anti-tank ditches on both its axes and plunged into a well-prepared defence in depth in a landscape of rocky, wooded ridges on the lower slopes of Mount Hermon.

Two brigades held this sector – one Syrian and the other Moroccan – supported by some 75 tanks. Built under Soviet supervision after the 1967 war, the Syrian defensive zone was up to 15km deep with closely integrated concrete bunkers linked by trenches. The zone was anchored on the right to Mount Hermon, and on the left to the impassable basalt rock Leja.

The northernmost Israeli spearhead was the 77th OZ Battalion of the 7th Armoured Brigade together with Task Force Amos, named after its commander, Lieutenant Colonel Amos Katz. The two battalions struck northeast beside the foothills of Mount Hermon towards Hader and Mazrat Beit Jan. Advancing a few kilometres to the south were the remnants of the Barak Brigade including Ben Hannan's force and the 74th Battalion, thrusting east through Jubat el Hashab to seize the commanding heights of Tel Shams. The Moroccan brigade with its integral tank battalion was facing the 77th Battalion, while to its south were the disorganised remnants of the Syrian 7th Infantry Division. By late afternoon, the northern axis of the 7th Armoured Brigade controlled the Hader crossroads. On the morning of 12 October it beat off a counter-attack and, resuming its advance, took Mazrat Beit Jan after a six-hour battle. The southern wing of Eitan's advance also made steady progress and the vital Maatz crossroads were taken on Friday morning. At this point, Ben Gal ordered Ben Hannan to take Tel Shams, a rocky outcrop that overlooked the road to Damascus. However, he did not inform Eitan of this decision. This proved to be a costly mistake, prompted by a conviction that the Syrians were on the point of collapse and also by the IDF's lingering reliance on the use of armour alone. Since 1967, the IDF had reduced the organic infantry and artillery elements of its armoured formations. This erosion of the infantry strength led to the attack on Tel Shams being made by tanks alone.

With two companies providing supporting fire, Ben Hannan led a force – some 20 tanks strong – along a path that ran through the rocky perimeter of the Syrian position to take it from the rear. Initially Ben Hannan achieved surprise: the Syrian armour at the base of the position was overwhelmed at close range and eight of Ben Hannan's tanks broke through. Tel Shams was now under Israeli artillery fire and Ben Hannan ordered two of his tanks, covered by the remaining two, to claw their way to the summit. Now they came under Syrian anti-tank fire that knocked out four of Ben Hannan's tanks and sent the two survivors scrambling down the Tel. Ben Hannan himself was blown out of his turret and seriously injured. After darkness had fallen, he was rescued by a group of Israeli paratroops commanded by Captain Jonathon 'Yoni' Netanyahu, later to lead the famous Entebbe raid. Tel Shams was to remain in Syrian hands until the night of 13 October, when the 31st Parachute Brigade captured it with minimal casualties.

To the south, Laner's division, comprising the 17th and 679th Reserve Armoured Brigades and the 9th Reserve Armoured Brigade, transferred from Peled's command, began its attack at 1300hrs on 11 October. Once again over-reliance on the use of unsupported armour in the thrust down the road to Damascus led to trouble when the Israelis encountered a well-co-ordinated Syrian defence. At the Khan Arnaba crossroads, the 17th Reserve Armoured Brigade, led by Colonel Ran Sarig, came under heavy artillery and Sagger ATGW fire. Tanks at the rear of the column ran into minefields when they left the road. The 17th Reserve Armoured Brigade was reduced to just five tanks.

Laner ordered the 9th Reserve Armoured Brigade south through Jaba, intending to bypass the crossroads, but that night Syrian infantry

A *Sho't* advances at speed towards the frontline. The *Sho't* or Upgraded Centurion can be identified from the front by the revised US-style headlight clusters and the fire extinguisher pull-handle above the spare track links. The *Sho't* proved to be the outstanding tank of the October War and fundamental to the Israeli victory over Syria.

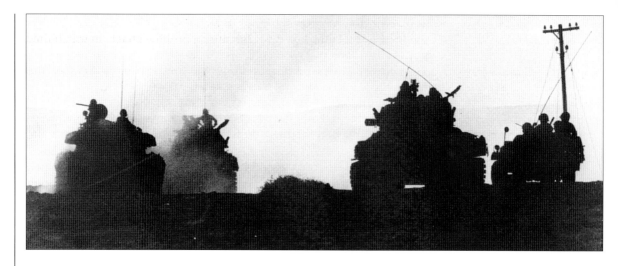

counter-attacked through the lava beds, cutting off the Israeli units at Khan Arnaba. An attempt to drive them off with armour resulted in more losses and underlined the vulnerability of unsupported tanks to determined attack by infantry armed with RPG-7s. The situation was retrieved by an attached paratroop battalion, which mopped up the Syrians and evacuated the Israeli wounded. The paratroopers were shocked by the exhausted condition of the surviving tank crews, begging them to rest and taking over the job of refuelling and re-arming their vehicles.

On the morning of 12 October, Laner decided to bypass Khan Arnaba with a wide outflanking movement to the south through Nasej towards Knaker that would avoid the Leja lava country blocking his path. His aim was to take Sasa on the Damascus road from the south and to establish a line within 30km of the city to bring the Syrian capital within range of the IDF's heavy artillery. That afternoon, while the 679th Reserve Armoured Brigade replenished, the 17th and 9th Reserve Armoured Brigades joined forces to drive east, watched by Laner from his forward headquarters at Tel Shaar, which provided sweeping views of the Syrian plain. It seemed as if the Syrians were broken and now unable to offer further resistance west of Damascus.

While observing his troops advance, Laner noticed huge dust clouds some 10km to his south. A major armoured formation was deploying for action. Laner's first reaction was that the dust had been raised by some of Peled's formations, but Hofi informed him that Peled was still in position. Hofi had transferred another of Peled's units, the 205th Reserve Armoured Brigade, to Laner's command, but this was due to arrive from a completely different direction. In fact, the approaching armour was that of Iraq's 3rd Armoured Division, two armoured brigades and a mechanised brigade with a combined total of some 180 tanks. Laner ordered the 679th Reserve Armoured Brigade, refuelling near Nasej, to deploy to the south. The 205th Reserve Armoured Brigade, assigned from Peled's division, was deployed between Tel Maschara and Tel el Mal. The 17th and 9th Reserve Armoured Brigades were to return from Knaker and take up positions facing south.

The Iraqis had blundered into an armoured battle for which they were in no way prepared. Their arrival was certainly fortuitous but they

**As dusk falls, Shermans and Centurions of the 9th Reserve Armoured Brigade advance up the Gamla Rise to engage Syrian tanks approaching the edge of the escarpment overlooking Israel proper. The prompt deployment of Israeli tank reserves in single companies rather than complete battalions or larger formations was crucial in stemming the Syrian onslaught.**

were incapable of exploiting the opportunity. Laner anticipated that the Iraqis would attack at dusk, but after a probing attack, in which they lost 17 tanks, the Iraqis then halted, awaiting the arrival of the division's second armoured brigade. Early on the morning of 13 October the Iraqis advanced northward into the area between Maschara and Nasej.

Laner had deployed his four brigades in an 'open box' formation, the northern side of which was formed by the 9th and 679th Reserve Armoured Brigades deployed east of Jaba at the foot of Tel Shaar; the east side of the box was provided by the 17th Reserve Armoured Brigade in a line running north–south through Nasej; the west side of the box was formed by the 205th Reserve Armoured Brigade, deployed along the Maschara–Jaba Road

The Iraqis remained unaware of the trap into which they were blundering. As they approached the foot of Tel Shaar they were about to run straight into 200 tanks and about 50 artillery pieces. The Israelis waited until first light, when the Iraqis had approached to within 275m before the Super Sherman tanks of 19th Brigade opened fire. The effect of the concentric fire of four armoured brigades was devastating. The Iraqi 8th Mechanised Brigade was destroyed in a matter of minutes. 80 Iraqi tanks were knocked out and the remainder fled in disorder. Not one Israeli tank was hit. The brief and disastrous Iraqi intervention, however, had an effect on the overall picture. It enabled the Syrians to move a brigade north to block the approach to Damascus, which they would not have been able to do had not the hapless Iraqi armoured formations briefly occupied a major part of the front. The principal role in the defence of Damascus was assigned to the Syrian 3rd Armoured Division, which remained relatively fresh and battleworthy when given

**Israeli fitters replace the front idler wheel of a damaged *Sho't* in the field. Working around the clock, the repair teams of the Israeli Armoured and Ordnance Corps played a vital part in restoring battle-damaged equipment to operational use. Their tireless efforts were fundamental to the eventual Israeli victory.**

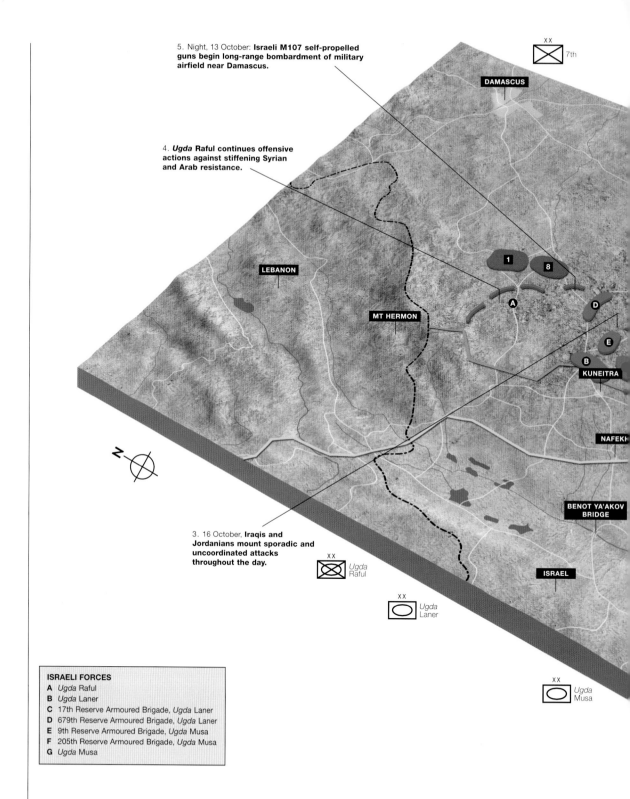

5. Night, 13 October: **Israeli M107 self-propelled guns begin long-range bombardment of military airfield near Damascus.**

4. *Ugda* **Raful continues offensive actions against stiffening Syrian and Arab resistance.**

3. 16 October, **Iraqis and Jordanians mount sporadic and uncoordinated attacks throughout the day.**

DAMASCUS

7th

LEBANON

MT HERMON

KUNEITRA

NAFEKH

BENOT YA'AKOV BRIDGE

ISRAEL

*Ugda* Raful

*Ugda* Laner

*Ugda* Musa

**ISRAELI FORCES**
A  *Ugda* Raful
B  *Ugda* Laner
C  17th Reserve Armoured Brigade, *Ugda* Laner
D  679th Reserve Armoured Brigade, *Ugda* Laner
E  9th Reserve Armoured Brigade, *Ugda* Musa
F  205th Reserve Armoured Brigade, *Ugda* Musa
G  *Ugda* Musa

# LANER'S TRAP

13–17 October 1973, viewed from the south-west. Attacks by Iraqi 3rd Armoured Division and Jordanian 40th Armoured Brigade are beaten off with heavy losses by *Ugda* Laner. Meanwhile Israeli long-range artillery begins to bombard the suburbs of Damascus.

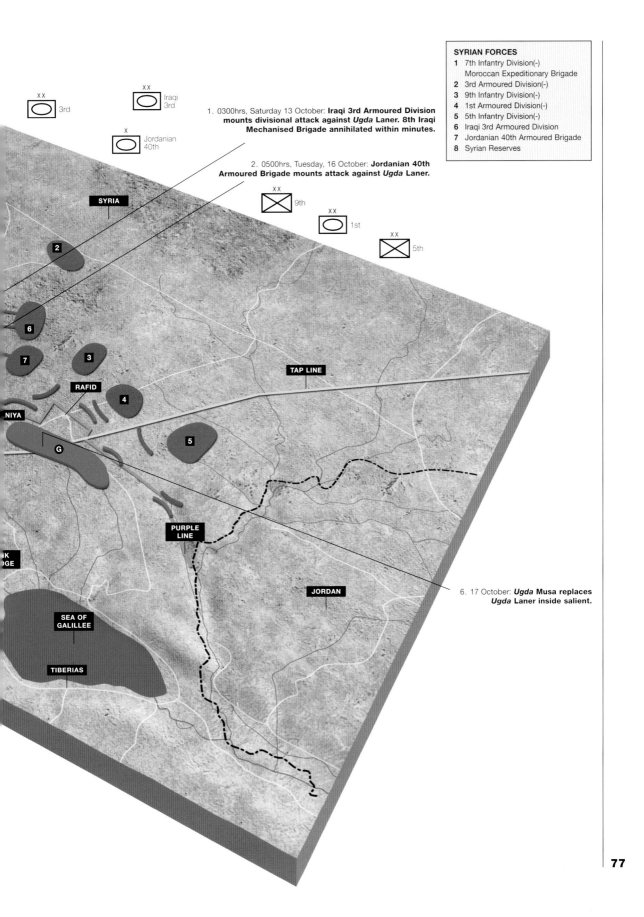

XX 3rd

XX Iraqi 3rd

X Jordanian 40th

SYRIA

1. 0300hrs, Saturday 13 October: **Iraqi 3rd Armoured Division mounts divisional attack against** *Ugda* **Laner. 8th Iraqi Mechanised Brigade annihilated within minutes.**

2. 0500hrs, Tuesday, 16 October: **Jordanian 40th Armoured Brigade mounts attack against** *Ugda* **Laner.**

XX 9th

XX 1st

XX 5th

**SYRIAN FORCES**
1 7th Infantry Division(-)
  Moroccan Expeditionary Brigade
2 3rd Armoured Division(-)
3 9th Infantry Division(-)
4 1st Armoured Division(-)
5 5th Infantry Division(-)
6 Iraqi 3rd Armoured Division
7 Jordanian 40th Armoured Brigade
8 Syrian Reserves

2

6

7

3

RAFID

NIYA

4

G

5

TAP LINE

PURPLE LINE

JORDAN

6. 17 October: *Ugda* **Musa replaces** *Ugda* **Laner inside salient.**

K GE

SEA OF GALILLEE

TIBERIAS

Centurion tanks of the Jordanian 40th Armoured Brigade deploy into attack formation prior to the offensive of 16 October. The attack failed because of the lack of support from their Iraqi and Syrian allies, but the superior tactical handling of Jordanian armour impressed the Israelis. Commanded by Colonel Haled Hajhouj al Majali, the 40th Armoured Brigade comprised some 150 tanks and 4,000 men. During the battle, the brigade sustained losses of 20 tanks and 100 casualties.

the task of holding the second Syrian defence zone around Sasa, which lay about midway between Kuneitra and the Syrian capital.

After administering a drubbing to the Iraqis, Eitan was ordered by Hofi to take in more ground to his right, leaving Laner free to monitor developments in the south. Eitan now had units of the Golani 1st Infantry Brigade at his disposal and these, in concert with paratroops, conducted tactical defence during the hours of darkness for the rest of the war. Some of the Western equipment they captured, including AML armoured cars, indicated that Saudi Arabian troops had entered the line. Meanwhile, Laner had identified the Syrian assembly area as a point 40km east of Rafid, known as the Great Leja. Accordingly, on 13 October he pushed out the 9th Reserve Armoured Brigade to capture two hills, Tel Antar and Tel el Alakieh, which gave dominating views of the Great Leja.

Also exerting a belated influence over the course of events was King Hussein of Jordan. Hussein had decided to enter the war on 9 October. With his General Staff, he had studied four options. The first was to launch a full-scale offensive across the River Jordan into Jordan's former territories on the West Bank while Israel was fighting on two fronts against Egypt and Syria; the second was to distract a portion of the IDF by making an essentially defensive demonstration east of the Jordan; the third option was to commit a limited Jordanian force to the battle in Syria, where it could fight under the Syrian SAM umbrella and air force; the last option was to sit tight and do nothing.

King Hussein was operating under a number of constraints, however, not least the weakness of the Jordanian air force and the absence of a modern air defence system. Nor did the Jordanian Army possess any anti-tank guided missiles and although one of the best-trained and motivated armies in the Arab world, it had little in the way of reserves and fielded mainly obsolescent equipment.

Moreover, by 9 October, Jordanian intelligence was telling Hussein that the Syrian offensive had failed, a development that ruled out his first option. But the political realities in the Arab world did not allow Hussein the luxury of inaction. He calculated that the Israelis would understand his position and would not take any reprisals if, while he remained inactive on the River Jordan front, he dispatched a contingent of Jordanian troops to fight in Syria. In this fashion he could combine a watered-down element of the second option – a demonstration on the Jordan – with the third, the despatch of a limited contingent to Syria. Hussein sent a retired Chief of Staff, Lieutenant General Amer Khammash, to Cairo to inform President Sadat of his decision.

On 13 October, the Jordanian 40th Armoured Brigade entered Syria. It comprised some 4,000 men, fielding 150 Centurion tanks and was commanded by Colonel Haled Hajhouj al Majali. That same day the 40th Armoured Brigade proceeded on the Damascus road through Deraa and then northwest to the frontline. That night, Israeli M107 175mm self-propelled artillery began to fire on the military airfield at Damascus, the start of an intermittent bombardment that would last for several days. It was augmented by IAF raids against Syrian air bases and industrial plants. During one of these raids two large Soviet heavy-lift aircraft were destroyed at Damascus' civil airport.

On 14 October, the Jordanian 40th Armoured Brigade entered the frontline just north of El Hara, between the Iraqi 3rd Armoured Division and the 9th Syrian Infantry Division on the south face of the Israeli salient. Promoted to Brigadier that day, Colonel Majali was placed under the command of Brigadier General Lafta, commanding the Iraqi 3rd Armoured Division on the eastern sector of the Arab line. On 15 October, Lafta's division was ordered to mount a major counter-attack the next day west of Kfar Shams that was to include the Jordanians and a brigade from the Syrian 9th Infantry Division. H-hour was set for 0500hrs but the Arab preparations were interrupted by a spoiling attack launched by Laner on the afternoon of the 15th.

At 0500hrs on 16 October the Jordanians moved on to the attack supported by an attached Saudi contingent and a Syrian brigade. The Iraqis chose not to join them. The Jordanians advanced on Tel Maschara but were halted by accurate fire from the 17th Reserve Armoured Brigade and withdrew having lost 20 of their Centurions. The Israelis noted that the Jordanian technical and tactical performances surpassed anything seen from the Syrians or the Iraqis. Some five hours later the Iraqis attacked Tel Antar and Tel-Alakieh but were driven off by the 17th Reserve Armoured Brigade. That morning, the Jordanian 40th Brigade was detached from the Iraqi 3rd Armoured and placed under the Syrian 9th Infantry Division. This produced a certain amount of bad-tempered bickering as Brigadier Majali outranked the Syrian commander of the 9th Infantry Division, Colonel Tourkmani. A general was rushed down from Damascus to act as liaison officer and smooth ruffled feathers. Over the next few days, the Iraqis and the Jordanians launched a series of ill-co-ordinated and abortive attacks. On several occasions these allies fired on each other's ground and air forces. The Iraqi Air Force's operations were beset by similar problems and a number of air battles were fought between the Arab allies. In the latter part of the war, the most serious offensive against Israeli positions was beaten off after a seven-hour battle with the loss of a further 60 Iraqi and 12 Jordanian tanks.

The vital Israeli OP on Mount Hermon that had been captured by Syrian commandos on the first day of the war was finally recaptured on the final day of the war. Approaching from over Lebanese territory, Israeli Air Force CH-53 helicopters, carrying only half the usual number of troops because of the high altitude, landed on the highest point of Mount Hermon some 240m (800ft) above the captured Israeli OP. The Golani infantrymen and paratroopers of the 31st Parachute Brigade attacked supported by a fearsome air and artillery bombardment and their own mortars. The Syrian defenders resisted gallantly throughout the night of 21/22 October until the position was finally overrun. Here members of the Golani Brigade relax atop Mount Hermon after recapturing the position.

On 17 October, a lull descended on the front, enabling Peled to relieve the exhausted Laner on the eastern and southern faces of the Israeli salient. Laner's troops transferred to Peled's old positions along the 1967 ceasefire line. To the north, meanwhile, Eitan was preparing for a renewed effort to retake Mount Hermon. Simultaneously, battalions were switched to the Sinai front along with the bulk of the IAF. The IDF was to make no further advances on the ground

This transfer of Israeli troops to the Sinai convinced the Syrians that they had a chance to regain the initiative. There were now few reserves left in Israel and the lull on the battlefield had given the Syrians the opportunity to reorganise and re-equip the formations that had been so badly battered in the earlier fighting. Now they had what they believed was a firm ring around the Israeli salient swelling inside Syria. Further allied Arab contingents had arrived and another Iraqi division was on its way to join the battle in the north, although some may have seen this as a mixed blessing.

A new offensive was planned to begin on 21 October, spearheaded by the Iraqi 3rd Armoured Division and 40th Jordanian Armoured Brigade. Once a breakthrough had been achieved, the 1st Syrian Armoured Division was to exploit northwards towards the Kuneitra–Damascus road to cut Israeli communications in front of Sasa. This plan might have looked convincing on a situation map but events on the ground were to take over.

On the afternoon of 20 October, the Iraqis announced that they were not ready and the attack was postponed until the 22nd. By now both sides were jockeying for position as the expected UN-imposed ceasefire loomed. The principal action of 21/22 October was the Israeli recapture of Mount Hermon, which had been taken by the Syrians on the opening day of the war. The Syrians held the mountain with two elite formations, one of paratroops and the other of Special Forces. Now the IDF planned to retake the position, and the Syrian OP that overlooked it, using the Golani Brigade and men of the 31st Parachute Brigade, who were to be air-dropped in to seize the Syrian positions.

The Golanis began to climb Mount Hermon as night fell on 21 October. Two columns ascended on foot and a third travelled in halftracks accompanied by tanks and engineers. For the Golanis on foot, burdened by weapons, ammunitions and supplies, the ascent was a supreme test of stamina. The Syrians, dug-in behind rocks and equipped with night sights and RPGs, put up a dogged resistance, but by 1100hrs on 22 October Mount Hermon was again in Israeli hands.

The paratroopers landed close to the Syrian OP and repulsed a heliborne counter-attack, downing three Syrian helicopters. They then overran the OP and began to move down the ridge to assist the Golanis. In the attack, the Golanis lost 51 killed and 100 wounded. A young Golani summed it up in a TV interview several days later: 'We were told that Mount Hermon is the eyes of the state of Israel and we knew we had to take it, whatever the cost.'

# AFTERMATH

On the evening of 22 October, the Syrians accepted a ceasefire proposed by the Security Council of the UN. Israel and Syria thereafter ceased further ground activity, although artillery fire continued from both sides for another 24 hours. On the night of 23 October, the shelling began to slow down and by midnight it had ceased altogether. Active combat operations on the Northern Front had come to a close with the Israelis having regained the ground they had lost during the war and also having taken control of a large additional portion of Mount Hermon, as well as the Sasa salient on the plain below.

It proved harder, in the aftermath of the October War, to secure an Israeli–Syrian agreement. The two nations did not sign a ceasefire agreement and for months the Syrians refused to provide the Israelis with a list of PoWs. Unlike their Egyptian allies, the Syrians declined to negotiate directly with the Israelis, or even to meet them. For their part the Israelis were willing to withdraw to the pre-October War Purple Line, but not prepared to cede part of the Golan on the terms demanded by Syria.

*Sho't* **Upgraded Centurion tanks withdraw from the Tel Shams area on 18 June 1973 in accordance with the terms of the ceasefire agreement brokered by the Security Council of the United Nations. (United Nations)**

*Sho't* **tanks withdraw through the ruins of Kuneitra on 25 June 1974, following the ceasefire agreement signed by the Israelis and Syrians on 31 May. (United Nations)**

The result was a niggling war of attrition by the Syrians against the IDF forces in the Israeli-occupied enclave in Syria characterised by intermittent artillery bombardments and sniping. In the spring of 1974, small-scale infantry engagements erupted over the control of Mount Hermon. President Assad, an unbending negotiator, calculated that the mounting IDF casualty list would sap Israeli morale and, in time, bring them to the negotiating table.

Henry Kissinger, the US Secretary of State, shuttled tirelessly between Damascus and Jerusalem and, on 31 May 1974, the Israelis and the Syrians signed an 'Agreement on Disengagement'. Israel agreed to withdraw from the Sasa salient, the Syrian Hermon and a thin strip of territory to the west of the old Purple Line. This area, with a little no-man's-land and some Syrian territory to the east, became a 'separation of forces zone' with a maximum width of eight kilometres to be held and patrolled by a 1,200-strong UN observer force. Included in the strip was the derelict town of Kuneitra. Syrian and Israeli forces were barred from this zone, although it was placed under Syrian administration. Nevertheless, this zone would prevent another surprise Syrian attack. The agreement, implemented in June 1974, also allowed for an exchange of prisoners of war.

The war cost Syria some 3,100 dead and 6,000 wounded. The Iraqis lost 278 killed and 898 wounded while the Jordanian figures for killed and wounded were, respectively 23 and 77. Israel's losses on the Golan front were some 772 killed, 453 wounded and 65 prisoners, including pilots. In the fighting the Syrians had lost 1,150 tanks, Iraq some 200 and Jordan about 50.

In preparing for the offensive, the Syrians had devoted considerable effort to the training of their army. In turn, their soldiers were confident in their military leadership, a new phenomenon in their history. This did not prove sufficient, however, when they were confronted with Israelis fighting for national survival. Both the 7th and 188th Armoured Brigades fought with extraordinary resolution until they were virtually

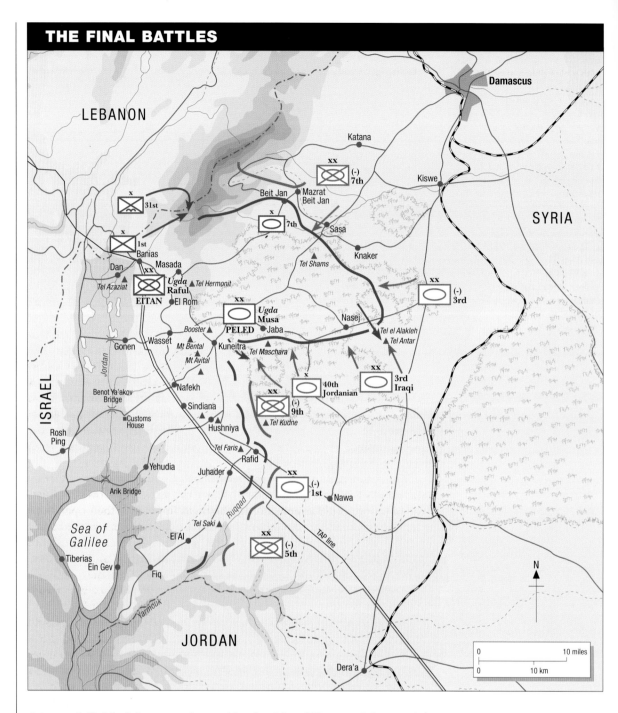

destroyed. Behind them was the cool leadership of Eitan and the crucial decision by Bar Lev and Elazar to give priority to the Northern Front.

Like their Egyptian allies, the Syrians were sufficiently realistic when planning the offensive to select limited and achievable objectives. By restricting their advance to the edge of the Golan escarpment, the Syrians acknowledged the vulnerability of their ground forces once they had left the protective umbrella of the SAMs. After his initial success on the Tap line road, which placed Syrian 1st Armoured Division within reach of Galilee, General Tlas failed to bring up any of his SAM-6 batteries and

The principal gallantry awards of the IDF are shown here with, from left to right, the *Ot Hamofet* with a blue ribbon awarded for distinguished and outstanding service in action. With its red ribbon, the *Ot Haoz* is Israel's second highest award for courage on the field of battle. Finally, the *Ot Hagvura* is Israel's highest award for supreme bravery on the field of battle. It equates to Britain's Victoria Cross or America's Medal of Honor. Unusually, its ribbon is yellow, a colour not normally associated with valour; but to the Jews it commemorates those who were forced to wear the yellow Star of David during the Middle Ages and under the yoke of the Nazi regime.

squandered the opportunity by committing his reserve tank division against strong opposition in the northern sector of the battlefield.

Indeed, although the Syrians achieved a strategic surprise on 6 October – the result of well-managed deception, Israeli intelligence failings and complacent assumptions by the IDF's high command – they failed to create a sufficient concentration of force for their opening attack. In contrast, the Israelis concentrated two of their three armoured divisions on a narrow front on the higher ground in the northern sector for their advance across the Ceasefire Line on 11 October.

Once they had recovered from the initial shock of the Syrian offensive, the Israelis achieved a satisfactory balance of forces. Their over-confident use of unsupported armour during the break-in phase of their operations, particularly during the assault on Tel Shams on 11 October, proved costly, however. Nevertheless, their armoured troops always had the edge on their Syrian enemy thanks to greater flexibility in tactics and command structures. The decision to commit reserve units by companies as soon as they had mobilised was crucial in turning the tide on the Golan, although it initially hampered the coherent tactical direction of the battle.

In the Syrian Army, co-operation between all arms was satisfactory. However, the same cannot be said for liaison between the Syrians and their Arab allies. Significantly, after the 1973 War, the Israelis incorporated mechanised infantry into its armoured corps and officers from both arms were cross-trained to deepen understanding of all-arms co-operation.

Co-operation between the Israeli Army and the IAF survived the initial battering that the latter received at the hands of Syrian SAMs and ZSU 'Shilkas'. The sacrifices made by the IAF in the first two days of the war played an important part in the holding of the Golan until reinforcements arrived. The October War demonstrated the colossal expenditure of ammunition and missiles characteristic of modern high-intensity warfare. Neither the Israelis nor the Syrians could have sustained the battle without massive airlifts from their superpower allies.

In purely military terms, the Israelis achieved a remarkable victory considering the dire conditions under which the IDF went to war. The

The IDF is sparing with gallantry medals and the highest honours are most often awarded posthumously. From the War of Independence in 1948 to the end of the October War, there have been only 41 recipients of the Medal of Valour, Israel's highest gallantry award, with 21 being awarded posthumously. Ten have gone to infantrymen and 13 to members of the armoured corps. Eleven were awarded during the October War. One recipient was Lieutenant Zwi 'Zwicka' Greengold for his remarkable actions along the TAP line road in the battles of the opening night of the war, when he fought continuously for 36 hours despite being severely wounded.

brilliant defensive battle fought by the 7th and Barak Armoured Brigades remains one of the most extraordinary feats of arms of the 20th century. It allowed the reservists to conduct a chaotic yet ultimately successful mobilisation despite the lack of many vital stores and the inability of units to obtain them. For instance, one reserve armoured brigade was delayed for nine hours in its deployment because there were insufficient fork-lift trucks to distribute the tank ammunition from the storage bunkers. Israeli overconfidence and the military intelligence assessment that war would not break out for several years had allowed the war reserve stores to become much depleted and often unfit for battle due to poor maintenance – the Israeli notion of '*yihyehbeseder*' or 'everything will be all right on the day' was a dangerous fallacy. This was compounded by inefficient administrative procedures and a sense of panic engendered by the overwhelming Arab offensives mounted simultaneously on two fronts. But to paraphrase Napoleon Bonaparte: 'In war, morale is to matériel by a factor of three to one'[3] and it was the superior morale and motivation of the average Israeli citizen/soldier that proved decisive in the end, with victory in both the Golan and Sinai campaigns.

By the same token, the October War of 1973 shattered the collective morale of Israeli society and for many victory was perceived as defeat. The price of the war in blood and treasure was too awful to contemplate – the financial costs were equivalent to the entire Israeli GNP for one year; the sacrifice of the dead and the suffering of the wounded incalculable. The certainties in the Israeli cause fostered since the foundation of the nation and a Jewish homeland in 1948 and the military victories thereafter were irrevocably lost after the war. The Agranat Commission that investigated the war ruptured the erstwhile Israeli self-confidence and sense of optimism in its destiny. The Labour government that had held sway for almost 30 years fell and with it many famous faces withdrew from public

---

**3** 'A la guerre, les trois quarts sont des affaires morales, la balance des forces réelles n'est que pour un autre quart.'
Correspondance de Napoléon 1er – 27 August 1808

On 6 June 1974, the United Nations Disengagement Observer Force comprising 1,200 troops from Austria, Canada, Peru and Poland took up positions in a buffer zone between the Israeli and Syrian forces from Mount Hermon in the north to the Jordanian border in the south. This allowed for the withdrawal of the IDF from their enclave inside Syrian territory. Here, M113 *Zelda* APCs move out from the Tel Shams area on 18 June 1974. (United Nations)

life. Politically, from a country that prided itself on achieving consensus democratically, Israel split into numerous mutually distrustful factions. Respect for authority was lost after the war and has never been fully regained, with the parties of neither the Left nor Right providing a coherent voice for the Israeli people either at home or abroad. With the supreme confidence, nay arrogance, of the pre-October War Israeli, Prime Minister Golda Meir declared in 1972: 'There is no such thing as a Palestinian problem.' Now there is little else. The October War of 1973 was a defining moment in the history of the Middle East. Ironically, in both Syria and Egypt, the 'Tashreen' War was perceived as a notable military success and a vindication of the Arab soldier on the battlefield. To the Israelis, the October War was a disaster from which they have never fully recovered. The image of an invincible IDF and the concept of a regional superpower were dispelled with Israel evermore dependent on the United States for military, diplomatic and economic support in the face of a hostile world.

# THE BATTLEFIELD TODAY

The Golan looks deceptively peaceful as you approach from the Israeli side; its steep escarpment dominates the reclaimed marshland and the low rolling hills of Galilee. At first sight it is a place of rugged beauty. Waterfalls and forests lend it a deceptively pastoral air.

Look closer. See the basalt boulders that litter the terrain. The rocks are half-hidden in the undergrowth and provide an awkward footing. It is easy to twist or break an ankle ... or lose a tank track. Rocks are not the only danger; the Heights are dotted with minefields of various vintages and origins. Soil creep means the minefields are difficult to mark. It is reckless to the point of madness to move from the roads and tracks that have been cleared.

These signs of war are subtle. When I first went up on the Golan, the 1973 war had finished a couple of days previously and signs of battle were much more obvious. With a handful of other kibbutz volunteers, I hitched up to the heights in an ancient American half-track. Western war tourists, we hid from bored military police to make the journey.

**A lonely *Sho't* stands as a memorial on one of the firing ramps on the Booster position overlooking the Valley of Tears. This is a later version of the *Sho't* with attachment points for 'Blazer' reactive armour and redesigned exhaust outlets. Curiously it carries the markings of the 679th Reserve Armoured Brigade whose tanks did not occupy the Booster feature. (Marsh Gelbart)**

The memorial to *Chativa 679* – the 679th Reserve Armoured Brigade – commanded by Colonel Uri Orr of *Ugda* Laner. The Hebrew inscription reads 'We will remember and not forget'. (Marsh Gelbart)

Remnants of battle were all around. Not far into our journey we passed three seemingly intact T-62s alongside Route 91, which wriggled up the escarpment all the way from Galilee to the outskirts of Kuneitra, the former Syrian garrison town. The friendly reservists manning the half-track said they were nicknamed 'the monsters'. They are long gone. As we swung northwards past the farming co-operative of Ein Zivan, we saw other leftovers of conflict. A couple of Arab stone houses badly damaged by gunfire, next to them, three burnt-out Syrian BTR-152 wheeled APCs. Nearby an Israeli jeep, riddled with shrapnel, and surrounded by field dressings, scraps of bloodstained bandage and an infusion bottle. It was a sobering moment.

The upper Customs House on the old border between Syria and Palestine was the most westerly point reached by Syrian reconnaissance elements during the October War. (Marsh Gelbart)

A memorial to the 7th Armoured Brigade stands beside Route 87 with a simple text reading 'Memorial to the 7th Brigade – In Fire They Will Come'. The memorial includes a Centurion tank bearing the inscription *Sa'ar* or Storm – Camp Sa'ar was one of the armoured encampments near Nafekh during the October War. Sa'ar was also the name given to the 74th Battalion of the 188th Barak Brigade. Curiously, this Centurion is a Dutch model with a Meteor petrol engine – not the type used by the 7th Armoured Brigade during the October War. (Marsh Gelbart)

The battle fought in the Valley of Tears was fundamental to holding the Syrian armoured onslaught in the opening days of the October War. Today there is a memorial here to the 77th OZ Battalion and the 7th Armoured Brigade that fought one of the greatest defensive battles in the history of armoured warfare. Among a grove of trees dedicated to the 7th Armoured Brigade lies a battered T-62; a mute testament to the ferocity of the battle. (Marsh Gelbart)

Kuneitra was a revelation, fought over by two armies in 1967 and 1973, it had been largely flattened. Reputedly Israeli bulldozers inflicted further damage before the town was returned to Syria. There was little left to destroy. Kuneitra was as far as we got. We tried to go further, to see the site of the 7th Brigade's epic stand, but were turned back by the military.

That was then, what of now. Is there anything left to see? There is not a simple answer to this question. There are memorials and battle sites to visit, but the most dramatic are from the 1967 war. Many of the features that were so heavily contested in 1973 are closed military areas. There is currently a ceasefire between Syria and Israel, not peace.

So what is it like to visit the Heights today and what is there to see of interest for the military enthusiast? Four years ago I took the same road, Route 91, that my friends and I took almost 30 years ago. The trip starts by the River Jordan, at *Gesher Bnot Ya'akov* (The Bridge of the Daughters of Jacob). The Jordan itself, the border before 1967, is little more than a muddy stream. The bridge is in fact one of two battered Bailey bridges, the second hidden behind foliage, constructed in October 1973 to allow a greater volume of military traffic to cross.

The Golan escarpment looms above you, some 500m or so in height. Even as you start the journey upwards, reminders of war are still to be seen. A kilometre east of the bridge is a heavily battered cluster of buildings. Known as the Customs Houses, they used to be the frontier posts between the British Mandate of Palestine and French-controlled Syria. The bullet holes that riddle the buildings date back to 1967 when the Israelis stormed the Heights. In 1973, Syrian reconnaissance elements had reached to a few hundred metres east of the Upper Customs House before being pushed back. Just to the north of the Customs Houses is a set of deep Syrian bunkers captured in 1967 and left as a memorial. The bunkers survived heavy air attack; Israeli infantry had to clear them one by one. At the site of a preserved bunker, a look-out point known as *Mitzpeh Gadot* gives a wonderful view of the Galilee and Hula valley below. It is a clear reminder of the advantages of holding the high ground in any military conflict.

A battlefield remains a dangerous place long after hostilities cease. The Golan Heights in particular hold many dangers, from minefields and unexploded ordnance to restricted military areas and derelict military equipment such as this battered M51 Sherman.

If you continue along Route 91 about another four kilometres east from the Customs Houses there is a track to the left. Drive past an Israeli army camp and you will find the ruined Syrian village of Awinet. Shortly beyond Awinet, in a wooded area, is an abandoned Syrian Army base. This is sometimes used by the IDF for FIBUA (Fighting in built-up areas) training. Like so much of the Golan it is a closed military area. However, the natural beauty spots of Gilboa and Dvora waterfalls are open to the public. Turn back and head east along Route 91 to *Ha'shiryon* (Armour) junction and you reach Nafekh. Nafekh was Israel's HQ on the Golan. The HQ was overrun by the Syrians during the 1973 war, but they were not able to consolidate their hold before it was recaptured. Drive slowly past Nafekh and you will usually see clusters of *Merkava* tanks hidden amongst sparse woodland. Some six kilometres beyond Nafekh, is the large settlement of Ein Zivan. Turn northwards at Ein Zivan's road junction, take Route 98, and you will be heading towards a series of hills that dominate the surrounding plateaux. These hills, known locally as Tels, are the remains of extinct volcanoes. It was from around these hills – Booster, Avital, Bental and Hermonit – that the Israeli 7th Armoured Brigade broke the back of the Syrian offensive in 1973. All are still closed military areas, bristling with antennae. However, the northernmost Tel, Hermonit, is partly open to the public. There is a memorial to the 7th Brigade at Hermonit. A T-62 tank scarred by shell hits sits peacefully in a small grove of trees. Within view, but with no public access, are a number of firing ramps from which tanks can cover the rising valley below. This place was once a killing ground on a vast scale. It is part of Emek Bekaa, the Valley of Tears, in which so many Syrian tanks and their crews met their end in October 1973.

Kuneitra is back in Syrian hands and, of course, cannot be visited from the Israeli side of the border. Continue north along Route 98 to the junction with Route 99. Just before the junction is a track, marked 978. This leads to Mount Odem, and its look-out point. Mount Odem is the site of a large, sometimes occupied, bunker. If open, Mount Odem allows a great view of the surrounding area. If the track is closed, as it is when the bunker is occupied, don't even think of attempting the journey. Return to Route 98 as it spirals upwards to the vast bulk of Mount Hermon. In 1973 the snow-capped peaks of Hermon were fought over by Syrian and Israeli infantry, commandos and paratroops. He who controls Hermon is in command of much of the plateau below. The Israeli electronic listening station on Hermon is still there; you can look from a distance, perhaps from the ski runs that are found nearby. You cannot approach the station; it is one of the most sensitive and heavily guarded places in the Middle East.

If at Ein Zivan junction you turn south rather than north, you will travel through the area where Syrian armour broke through the Barak Brigade's defences. The terrain is still rugged but less hilly. Travel south-west towards the crocodile farm and hot springs of Hamat Geder. Before you cross the old border, there is a half-hidden memorial to the Barak Brigade. Faded wreaths of flowers are to be found alongside an upturned turret of a T-62, left as a reminder to the 7th Brigade's sacrifice.

The Golan Heights is contested ground. Currently it is quiet but it has been the focal point of fierce fighting. If you are going to visit, remember, it can be dangerous. Keep to cleared paths. Take a guided tour if you can. Never try to get into a closed military area. You may not live to regret your mistake. Road routes and numbers can change over time. What was open four years ago may be closed now. Use your common sense, there is much to see, but travel carefully.

Note: Neither the author nor the publishers of this book will be held liable for anyone visiting the battlefield and behaving in a way prejudicial to their own safety.

# FURTHER READING

The works of Chaim Herzog – *The War of Atonement: The Inside Story of the Yom Kippur War, 1973* (Weidenfeld and Nicholson 1975) and *The Arab-Israeli Wars: War and Peace in the Middle East* (Arms and Armour Press 1982) – are reliable sources from the Israeli point of view and must be seen as the semi-official history of the war. In both books, Israeli unit designations and IDF personnel names have been altered or abbreviated for security reasons. The reader is therefore referred to the works of Samuel M. Katz (see below).

For the political background to the October War and indeed all 20th century Arab-Israeli wars, Benny Morris has written an unsurpassed account in *Righteous Victims: A History of the Zionist–Arab Conflict 1881–1999* (John Murray 2000).

*The Yom Kippur War* by The Insight Team of *The Sunday Times* (Sunday Times 1974/Andre Deutsch 1975) was written immediately after the conflict but nevertheless gives an evocative contemporary coverage of the conflict with many interesting quotes from Israeli soldiers before the official version of the war was dictated by the IDF.

There are several excellent accounts of the ground-fighting in the Golan campaign, particularly *Israeli Tank Battles Yom Kippur to Lebanon* by Samuel M. Katz (Arms and Armour Press 1988) and his exciting history of the 7th Armoured Brigade, *Fire and Steel* (Pocket Books 1996) – both books are a must for anyone interested in the Israeli Armoured Corps. As a former member of the IDF, Sam Katz has undertaken considerable research into the campaign, and the unit designations of Israeli formations that he lists are used in this volume as being the most reliable to date.

The book *Chariots of the Desert: The Story of the Israeli Armoured Corps* by David Eshel (Brassey's 1989) is essential reading for any student of this campaign as Colonel Eshel was an eyewitness during the fierce battles on the Golan in the October War.

Lieutenant Colonel David Eshel (formerly of the Israeli Armoured Corps) also produced a series of monographs during the early 1980s on all aspects of the Arab-Israeli wars. The actual campaigns were recounted in a series called *Born in Battle* and analysis of the weapon systems appeared in *War Data* and *Military Enthusiast.* For the discerning reader, they contain a wealth of facts and photographs that deserve close scrutiny for their comprehensive coverage of the IDF and its history.

For a vivid first-hand account, the reader is strongly advised to consult Avigdor Kahalani's remarkable book *The Heights of Courage: A Tank Leader's War on the Golan* (Praeger 1992). Awarded Israel's highest gallantry decoration, the Medal of Valour, for his leadership and courage during the war, one can only read such a book with humility and wonder at the fortitude of the soldier under the most awful duress in high-intensity warfare. There is also an excellent account of the Golan campaign in the same author's autobiography *A Warrior's Way* (Steimatzky 1999).

Of all the books written about the October War during the 1970s, Colonel Trevor Dupuy's *Elusive Victory: The Arab-Israeli Wars 1947–1974* (Macdonald and Jane's 1978) must be considered the most comprehensive and impartial account of the Golan campaign. Its value lies in the fact that Dupuy was able to interview combatants of all the warring nations soon after the conflict to give the most balanced account of the campaign from the Arab perspective and the statistics he quotes are generally held to be the most accurate. However, its unit designations and names of personnel of the IDF are not correct, being subject to Israeli security consideration at the time of publication.

# INDEX

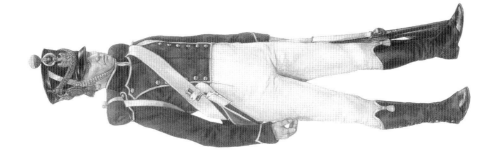

# FIND OUT MORE ABOUT OSPREY

❏ Please send me the latest listing of Osprey's publications

❏ I would like to subscribe to Osprey's e-mail newsletter

Title / rank

Name

Address

City / county

Postcode / zip                    state / country

e-mail

CAM

I am interested in:

❏ Ancient world
❏ Medieval world
❏ 16th century
❏ 17th century
❏ 18th century
❏ Napoleonic
❏ 19th century

❏ American Civil War
❏ World War 1
❏ World War 2
❏ Modern warfare
❏ Military aviation
❏ Naval warfare

Please send to:

**USA & Canada**:
Osprey Direct USA, c/o MBI Publishing, P.O. Box 1, 729 Prospect Avenue, Osceola, WI 54020

**UK, Europe and rest of world**:
Osprey Direct UK, P.O. Box 140, Wellingborough, Northants, NN8 2FA, United Kingdom

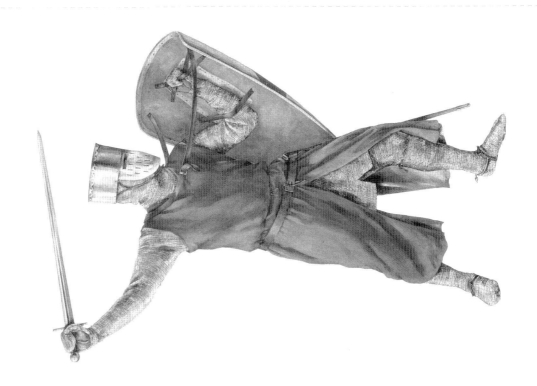

OSPREY PUBLISHING

www.ospreypublishing.com

call our telephone hotline
for a free information pack

USA & Canada: 1-800-826-6600
UK, Europe and rest of world call:
+44 (0) 1933 443 863

**Young Guardsman**
Figure taken from *Warrior 22:
Imperial Guardsman 1799–1815*
Published by Osprey
Illustrated by Richard Hook

POSTCARD

**Knight, c.1190**
Figure taken from *Warrior 1: Norman Knight 950 – 1204 AD*
Published by Osprey
Illustrated by Christa Hook